The Key

to Effective
Spiritual Growth

*A Believer's Guide
to the Christian Journey*

Jean T. Saint Sauveur

TEACH Services, Inc.
P U B L I S H I N G
www.TEACHServices.com • (800) 367-1844

World rights reserved. This book or any portion thereof may not be copied or reproduced in any form or manner whatever, except as provided by law, without the written permission of the publisher, except by a reviewer who may quote brief passages in a review.

The author assumes full responsibility for the accuracy of all facts and quotations as cited in this book. The opinions expressed in this book are the author's personal views and interpretations, and do not necessarily reflect those of the publisher.

This book is provided with the understanding that the publisher is not engaged in giving spiritual, legal, medical, or other professional advice. If authoritative advice is needed, the reader should seek the counsel of a competent professional.

Copyright © 2017 Jean T. Saint Sauveur

Copyright © 2017 TEACH Services, Inc.

ISBN-13: 978-1-4796-0777-8 (Paperback)

ISBN-13: 978-1-4796-0778-5 (ePub)

ISBN-13: 978-1-4796-0779-2 (Mobi)

Library of Congress Control Number: 2017907304

Unless otherwise indicated, Scripture quotations are taken from the King James Version. Other versions used are

The American Standard Version (ASV), published in 1901 by Thomas Nelson & Sons. Douay Rheims. Berean Study Bible (BSB) © 2016 by Bible Hub and Berean.Bible. Used by Permission. All rights Reserved. *Complete Jewish Bible* (CJB) © 1998 by David H. Stern. Published by Jewish New Testament Publications, Inc. All rights reserved. Used by permission. *The Holy Bible, English Standard Version*® (ESV). © 2001 by Crossway Bibles, a publishing ministry of Good News Publishers. All rights reserved. *GOD'S WORD*® is a copyrighted work of God's Word to the Nations. Quotations are used by permission. © 1995 by God's Word to the Nations. All rights reserved. *The Holy Bible: International Standard Version*® (ISV). Release 2.1. © 1996–2012 The ISV Foundation. All rights reserved internationally. Louis Segond Bible. Public domain. *The Holy Bible, New Living Translation* (NLT). ©1996, 2004, 2007. Used by permission of Tyndale House Publishers, Inc., Carol Stream, Illinois 60188. All Rights Reserved. *The Original Aramaic New Testament in Plain English with Psalms & Proverbs*. © 2007, 8th edition, © 2013. All rights reserved. Used by Permission. *Revised Standard Version of the Bible* (RSV), © 1952 [2nd edition, 1971] by the Division of Christian Education of the National Council of the Churches of Christ in the United States of America. Used by permission. All rights reserved. *New American Standard Bible* (NASB). © 1960, 1962, 1963, 1968, 1971, 1972, 1973, 1975, 1977, 1995 by The Lockman Foundation, La Habra, Calif. All rights reserved. *The Living Bible* (TLB). © 1971 by Tyndale House Foundation. Used by permission of Tyndale House Publishers Inc., Carol Stream, Illinois 60188. All rights reserved. *La Bible d'étude Semeur* [Study Bible of the Sower]. © 1992, 1999 by Biblica, Inc.® Used by permission. All rights reserved worldwide. Weymouth New Testament. Public domain.

This book is designed to be a guide for the Christian journey.

This book is designed to be a guide for the Christian journey. It can also be viewed as a mirror reflecting the state of Christian growth. It will allow readers to conceptualize and understand in themselves and in the world around them many things that have been obscure.

"As strangers and pilgrims," "you search the scriptures, because you think that in them you have eternal life; and it is they that bear witness to" Jesus (1 Peter 2:11; John 5:39, RSV).

TABLE OF CONTENTS

PREFACE 9
INTRODUCTION. 11
   The letter to the Romans the heart of the plan of salvation.

Chapter 1 15
GOD IS LOVE

   The incomprehensible love of God—God's use of the image of the mother—God's use of the image of the father—God's use of the image of the bride and groom—The power of agapē love—How to acquire agapē love—To love is the essential thing

Chapter 2 28
THE WORD OF GOD IS POWERFUL

   The power of God's word—Jesus defined His mission—Jesus gives us power of attorney in His name—Jesus' focus on essential things—Jesus' power over sickness and death

Chapter 3 41
THE PROPHECIES, A DIVINE SIGNATURE

   Remarkable prophecies in Daniel 2, 4, and 5—The prophetic accuracy of the word of God—God limited the human lifetime by His word—When God speaks

Chapter 4 49
THE DIVINE REVELATION
> Divine revelation is a gradual process—Gradual education through consecration—Gradual education by the law—The prophecy of Daniel 2 and its progressive aspect—Baptism and its progressive implications—Extra-biblical revelations—Mathematics of vertigo—The mimicry of sun and moon—The captivating moon.

Chapter 5 64
A CONTAGIOUS SIN
> The definition of sin—The contagious sin of Adam and Eve—Sin, a binding force in the natural man—The depravity of the human race—The flesh, the abode of sin—The destruction of the flesh—The antidote to sin, the cross, or the death of the "old man"—The solution to sin—the blood of Jesus Christ—Sin, a crucial issue for the believer—Clarification

Chapter 6 77
DYING TO THE LAW
> The role of the law of God—The law and the unfolding of the plan of salvation—When are we under the law, according to Paul?—Dying to sin and living for God in Christ—How to be released from the grip of the law, according to Paul—Clarification

Chapter 7 89
THE CROSS
> The meaning of the cross in the life of the believer—The cross, the foundation of Christianity—The role of the cross or difficulties—Carrying one's cross to follow Jesus—Everyone has his cross and path—God transforms us through difficulties—The cross is the path of glory

Chapter 8 103
THE NEW BIRTH
> The resurrection or the new birth—The heart—A grafted creature—The human race in Jesus Christ—Jesus Christ in believers—A successful graft—Clarification

Chapter 9 113
TRANSFORMED CHRISTIANS
>The fruit of the new birth—The Christian and self-control—Healthy limbs form a healthy body—Living as Christian priests—A person with the perfect stature of Christ

Chapter 10 122
THE BAPTISM OF THE HOLY SPIRIT
>The Holy Spirit in the life of the Christian—The seal of God on the Christian—The baptism of the Holy Spirit—The Holy Spirit before baptism—The Holy Spirit and the prophets—The roles of the Holy Spirit—Why we should not grieve the Holy Spirit—The sadness of the Holy Spirit—Reasons for His sadness—Compelling facts—Going further

Chapter 11 136
THE CHRISTIAN SOLDIER
>The soldier's work—Developing combat techniques—The Christian's weapons are spiritual—The power of our weapons—Exploring the faith—The significance of faith—Pitfalls to faith—The prayer of faith, a formidable weapon

Chapter 12 149
AN EXTRAVAGANT DESTINATION
>The glorious return of Christ—Prophetic announcements regarding Christ's return—Reasons for Christ's return—Characteristics of Christ's return—Promises for the saved—The true home of the believer: The Father's house—The New Jerusalem—Exploring the New Jerusalem

PREFACE

The plan of salvation is like a great canvas that God unfolds progressively before us across the centuries and generations. Due to the shortness of the life of man, no one person can appreciate all the beauty of the completion of this work, which has been painted with dexterity by distinguished artists. It is up to the last generation to contemplate all the finesse and excellence of this skillfully conceived and jealously preserved depiction, under the watchful eye of the Artist-in-Chief, the Creator God.

The writing of this book was not something I had planned to do, even though I had been ruminating on the idea for years. It was the result of a conversation I had with my wife who expressed her desire that I write a book about prayer and praise. The next day, I started drafting a table of contents and brainstorming ideas for the project. Little by little, I have put them in order, refining them to produce this book to contribute to your spiritual fulfillment.

The Bible is an immense and inexhaustible library. After centuries and generations, we have not reached the depths of research and new branches of study available. With all our efforts, it seems that we are just beginning to search this treasure buried in the depths of God. What is more wonderful in our study of the Bible is that the Holy Spirit reveals to us certain mysteries and truths that have escaped our grasp until now.

Accurate knowledge of the Word of God can give us clear ideas and help us make wise choices for our spiritual future. Misinformation or a lack of biblical knowledge can unwittingly lead us onto the path of perdition (Hosea 4:6). I dare to believe, above all, that this work will continue to tear the veil that for too long has held us blind to certain truths, making room for greater light.

"A book," says Victor Hugo in his *Intellectual Autobiography*, "is like the gearing of a machine. Have a care of these black lines on white paper; they are forces; they combine, compose, decompose, enter into one another, pivot upon one another, unwind, interknit, embrace, act. That line bites, that line binds and grips, that line attracts, that line subdues. Ideas are like gearing. You feel yourself drawn by the book. It will not let go of you until it has given a certain shape to your mind." I assume that this book will help you experience new positive emotions in your relationship with God.

As judged by what it reveals about the plan of salvation, it is the best work that I can put at your disposal. I hope you will find, as you might on a freshly explored beach, valuable materials to use in building your personal temple and pretty shells to embellish the inside. The production of this book was a surprise. Will there be another? The answer is uncertain, although I will not stop digging into the Word of God in search of hidden treasures.

Jean T. Saint Sauveur

INTRODUCTION

In April of 2014, I participated in a forum called to promote the spread of the good news of salvation. In one exchange, I remarked to a speaker that Christians lack an effective guide book for the spiritual journey. Indeed, some of us have spent years in church without really grasping the guidelines for an effective spiritual journey, guidelines that would be either beacons or compasses to keep us on the path to eternal life. The book that you are reading today is an outgrowth of this exchange. I have spent considerable time searching the Scriptures to find the main way to salvation. I am pleased to say that I have found it! This book traces the main itinerary of the Christian journey. In that journey, there will be particular problems for the Holy Spirit to help each person solve. Dealing with these individual problems is like leaving the highway for a time and pursuing a stretch of back road, though eventually returning to the main roads and passing through the key checkpoints. For this reason, we cannot compare conversion to an exact science like 2 + 2 = 4. However, it is clear, from Jesus' conversation with Nicodemus about conversion in John 3 and the apostle Paul's statement about spiritual growth in 1 Corinthians 3:1, 2, that there is a course that the life of each Christian must take that corresponds to the analogy of the Christian journey. The travelers are not merely to go in a general direction without trajectory or rules and without a defined objective.

In the Christian journey, the believer must be baptized with water and with the Holy Spirit according to Jesus Christ' instructions (Matt. 28:19; Acts 1:5). This book describes, in minute detail, what water baptism and the baptism of the Holy Spirit represent as an experience. It will give you the fundamental secrets derived from Jesus' conversation with Nicodemus, a doctor of the law who could not understand what the Lord Jesus was saying. Reading this book, you will discover the visible signs of the baptism of the Holy Spirit. You will come to understand how the carnal man must die before receiving the new birth. It will explain what Jesus meant when He said that the believer must "take up his cross and follow" Him (Matt. 16:24; Mark 8:34; Mark 10:21; Luke 9:23). It will outline what to expect in the Christian life and present, from Scripture, God's means of spiritual education. It will answer when it is that a Christian is no longer under the law.

> *The exposition of Paul in the Epistle to the Romans shows that he was at the peak of his literary art and that the Holy Spirit had revealed to him the mysteries of the plan of salvation.*

This book also describes the unfailing love of our Creator for humankind and the supreme revelation of that love in the person of Jesus Christ. It emphasizes the images that are used to express His attachment to the church. The exposition of Paul in the Epistle to the Romans shows that he was at the peak of his literary art and that the Holy Spirit had revealed to him the mysteries of the plan of salvation. This book aims to enable you to identify the Christian's powerful weapons of combat and begin using them to protect yourself against the assaults of the evil one. It has been designed to encourage your walk in sanctification.

The work you hold is the fruit of my personal experiences and the result of my journey in understanding the will of God for Christians. I do not write out of habit but from an urgency to share with you knowledge that is often obscure, despite its importance for spiritual progress. It is, in fact, our heavenly Father's longing that He have a multitude of children transformed into the image of His dear Son, Jesus Christ, forming a kingdom of priests, of which Christ is High Priest and Sovereign. This means that He has made available all the elements our spiritual condition requires to accomplish His will. Let us strive, my brothers and sisters, as do athletes in the Olympic games who expend all their energy to gain a passing medal. Victory is within our reach if we look up to Jehovah as Moses did in defeating Amalek (Exod. 17:16), by keeping our hands raised to the throne of the Lord. In this way, we will win the great final victory. This experience reminds us of the importance of remaining in communion with God through prayer in sanctification in order to defeat the enemy.

The Letter to the Romans the Heart of the Plan of Salvation

Understanding the Epistle to the Romans will help believers live a more fulfilling Christian life as they grasp a fuller revelation of the plan of salvation. Sometimes sincere Christians, animated by goodwill, lead a miserable spiritual life because they have a distorted perception of the will of God. In various facets of our lives, knowledge can enhance our capacity to act and react, either spontaneously or in anticipation. On pages 69 and 70 of Alfred Kuen's Letters of Paul, the author praises the letter to the Romans, backing his praise by the glowing recommendations of other authors. We wish to emphasize the importance of this letter in the heart of the New Testament, for we will use several passages from it to corroborate the truths presented in this book. We will begin by speaking briefly about the importance of Romans for the understanding of sacred Scripture. Some writers assert that this epistle represents Paul's last will and testament. In this epistle, the apostle left his readers the secrets of the heart of the plan of redemption. According to Alfred Kuen, Martin Luther considered Romans to be "the chief part of the New Testament and the very purest Gospel" and "the heart and the marrow of all the books."

The epistle to the Romans expresses with the greatest precision what the Christian is in Jesus Christ, what God has done for each Christian in Jesus Christ, and what each Christian should be in Jesus Christ. It is sometimes called "the golden key of the Scriptures." When church leaders take Romans as the divine word of the Holy Spirit to transform hearts, it can result in the renewal of the Christian communities they represent. Speaking of Romans, Robert Haldame wrote: "It is the part of Scripture which contains a detailed and systematic exhibition of the doctrines of Christianity. The great truths which are embodied and inculcated in every other part of the Bible, are here brought together in a condensed and comprehensive form" (*Exposition of the Epistle to the Romans*, p. 6). According to Alfred Kuen, John Calvin said: "If we have gained a true understanding of this Epistle, we have an open door to all the most profound treasures of Scripture."

The following exercise aims to pique your curiosity about the contents of the epistle to the Romans, which Pastor C. Den Boer called the "storm of the Holy Spirit," so that you will choose to spend more time picking up the treasures buried deep in every verse, sentence, and word of this "golden key of the Scriptures." As such, we might add that the golden key to the epistle itself is undoubtedly chapter 7. Let us drink deeply from this epistle to satisfy our thirst and carry us to new horizons.

Jean T. Saint Sauveur

Chapter 1
GOD IS LOVE

There is no higher revelation of God than that found in the first epistle of John: "And we have known and believed the love that God hath to us. *God is love*; and he that dwelleth in love dwelleth in God, and God in him" (1 John 4:16, emphasis added). Let us contemplate God's love.

The Incomprehensible Love of God

In a compilation entitled, *Children's Letters to God*, Stuart Hample and Eric Marshall reported the following letter, written by a little girl named Nan:

> Dear God, I bet it is very hard to love everyone in the whole world. There are only 4 people in our family, and I'm having a hard time loving all of them.
>
> Nan.

The story of a mother and her son, as told by Doris Hays Northstrom, provides a response to Nan's perplexity. In all, the mother in the story had three grown children. They enjoyed many wonderful gatherings together.

They picnicked and played volleyball in the back yard; they contemplated the beauties of nature on outings in natural settings. They lived a happy life together until, Brian, the youngest son, who was an affectionate, tender person, who loved his family, began succumbing to depression. At his school, the young man played volleyball. He also organized small competitions for his nieces and nephews. He was very close to his mother. Yet, at sixteen years of age, depression overtook him. He abandoned everything—school, family, and friends—to escape into the streets.

Brian's mother said that she did not stop encouraging her son or praying for him. One winter, he returned home and told his mother: "Mom, I'm scared. The world is so ugly." She rocked her 6'3" son in her arms, sweat mingled with tears running down his cheeks. She could smooth Brian's hair but not his pathway. "Brian," she said, "you're going to come through this hard time. The world needs a boy like you." The tormented young man left home again, and his mother continued to suffer in silence during long, dark days and sleepless nights. After a few weeks, Brian called his mother and said: "Mom, do you think I could come back? It's awful here. I think I'm going crazy. Can we meet to talk?"

The mother drove off at full speed to meet her son at the agreed upon restaurant. There she looked at her son, sitting with hollow eyes and haggard face, tired and lost, resembling that of an "old man." The painful appearance of her son shook her already tired heart. "I'm so confused," he said. "My head feels like it will explode."

Months passed, and then Mother's Day arrived. After a day of playing with her other children and her grandchildren, the mother heard a knock at the door. It was Brian, with his face thin and clothes wrinkled and stale. "I had to come," he said. "I couldn't let Mother's Day go by without letting you know I'm thinking of you." He handed her two pink carnations with a card that had these words: "Mom, I love you, and you're thought of more often than you'll ever know." The mother wrapped her arms around him, and he added, "Mom, I wanted to take my life and be through with the pain, but I could never do that to you." They cried together tears of mingled pain and joy. This time, Brian did not go away. Ten years later, he was still at home and doing well.

Rabindranath Tagore wrote: "I do not love him because he is good but because he is my child." His words echo what God's response to Nan's quandary could be. Our God loves us because we are His children whom He created according to His image and likeness. Through the work of redemption of Jesus Christ, the "whole treasury of heaven is open to those He seeks to save. Having collected the riches of the universe, and laid open the resources of infinite power, He gives them all into the hands of Christ, and says, All these are for man" (E. G. White, *The Desire of Ages*, p. 57).

The Creator God is the absolute Lord of all the universe. He is not limited in time and space. He is eternal, omniscient, and omnipresent. His greatness and wisdom cannot be grasped by the limited understanding of man. The finite cannot contain the infinite. To make Himself understood, He uses our language and our reality. God is love in His being and in His nature, even as He remains hostile to sin. All His words, all His actions are guided by love. Love is His dominant characteristic, and it determines what He does. Indeed, the Bible is the most beautiful love story within our grasp. It is so unassuming that it passes for an ordinary book, while its importance passes unnoticed. It is true that it contains scenes of violence, corruption, sin, and even political intrigue. However, these dark notes explain the existence of a cosmic struggle in which man is often caught in Satan's trap, while God seeks constantly to deliver him. The various stories of the Bible, which expose the imperfections of humanity, are evidence that the Creator cares about human misfortune and always reaches out to rescue those sinking into the mud of sin. It is the book par excellence, and it expresses the character of the Creator God. The Bible contains many miraculous interventions of God in His efforts to carry out His plan of love in order to free man from the chain of sin and reinstate him as His child.

> *The various stories of the Bible, which expose the imperfections of humanity, are evidence that the Creator cares about human misfortune and always reaches out to rescue those sinking into the mud of sin.*

This brief history will serve to give us a pale idea of what God felt at the time of the degradation of man whom He created in His image, according to His likeness, and to whom He gave dominion over all other creatures living on earth (Gen. 1:26–28).

We can imagine the disappointment of the king who saw one of his sons despise his royal rank to lead a life of debauchery and delinquency.

As far as possible, let us put ourselves in the monarch's shoes and consider the social and political implications of his son's disappointing choice. Earthly kings might try to get rid of their shame and restore their royal reputation by disowning or even eliminating their sons. However, instead of eliminating His rebellious children, God has made the ultimate sacrifice, sending His only begotten Son, Jesus Christ (John 3:16), to restore His image in us. In this way, He redeemed and restored the life of every son and daughter of Adam who accepts this sacrifice as a means of salvation. Today, Jesus Christ is our great Elder Brother, with whom we share the same Father (see Rom. 8:29).

God's Use of the Image of the Mother

God Almighty made an encompassing declaration to Moses about His love: "The LORD, the LORD, the compassionate and gracious God, slow to anger, abounding in love and faithfulness" (Exod. 34:6, NIV). In this statement, God used the Hebrew word *rachûhm*. The word means "full of compassion" and "merciful," a deep affection for a person, as one might feel for a son caught in a desperate situation—the affection a mother feels for her child. So the person who is moved feels pain, which comes from compassion in seeing his or her loved one suffering misery or calamity. This word can be attributed only to God in relation to man. The Hebrew word *rachûhm* is related to the word *râcham*, which means "bowels, belly, womb," or, by extension, "compassion," because it pictures compassion like that which a mother feels for her fetus in her womb, where her baby is forming in safety. In the Hebrew language, people who are slow to get angry are said to be "long of nose" (see Ps. 103:8; Prov. 14:29)—*'erekh apayim.*' This is because the nose allows a person to breathe fresh air more easily, refreshing their heart. Because of this, their nose takes time to blush when they are angry. Our God, our Father, used this idiom, or analogy, to tell us that He is slow to get angry. He is a Father who uses patience towards His children.

Another text that explains clearly and explicitly the love of God is the following: "Can a woman forget her sucking child, that she should not have compassion on the son of her womb? yea, they may forget, yet will I not forget thee" (Isa. 49:15). Without a concrete image from our earthly reality, we have great difficulty grasping the realities of the kingdom of God. This is why the Lord uses the example of a mother who loves her child to the extreme. After having nourished her child in the womb through the umbilical cord, the physical bond is replaced, at birth, by a powerful bond of love and unfailing affection. God knew that His use of this image would help us grasp a clearer representation of His love in that most of us have had the opportunity to experience maternal love.

The love that God has for us humans is without measure and without precondition. We are the object of His joy, His pleasure, and His concern. After the fall of man, the Lord did not wait to announce His plan to intervene for humankind by establishing a boundary between them and Satan (Gen. 3:15). He immediately announced His placing of a barrier of hostility between Satan and his progeny and the woman and hers. As a loving Father who is willing to offer all that He possesses for the benefit of His children, God issues promises to humankind that will multiply as they are fulfilled.

God's Use of the Image of the Father

The name "Almighty God" is the translation of the Hebrew word *El shaddai*, or *El shadday*. *El* in Hebrew means "God." *Shaddai* means "Almighty." Some commentators believe the term is based upon the ancient Babylonian word *sadû*, which means "breast" or "mountain." Others prefer the Hebrew root *sha*, which means "within the mother" [literally "breast of the mother"]. Thus, the word *shaddai* refers to God's paternal and maternal attributes. He is an Almighty God who has the means to fulfill all His promises. In addition to His unlimited might and power, He has the flexibility and tenderness of a nurturing mother to provide for the varying needs of His children. Genesis 49, verses 24 and 25, tells us: "But his bow abode in strength, and the arms of his hands were made strong by the hands of the mighty God of Jacob; (from thence is the shepherd, the stone of Israel:) even by the God of thy father, who shall help thee; and by the Almighty, who shall bless thee with blessings of heaven above, blessings of the deep that lieth under, blessings of the breasts, and of the womb."

The fulfillment of God's promises to His children continues to flow. He invites us to "possess ... the kingdom prepared for you from the foundation of the world" (Matt. 25:34, Douay-Rheims Bible). He created us to live in His presence. As a wise father who plans to have children, our heavenly Father made preparations for His offspring. After He had created heaven and earth, God organized it so that it could be inhabited and managed by man. To His great disappointment, His initial plan failed. Nonetheless, out of love for us, He has put into execution a second plan in which He can restore His image in us. Like the Jewish people traveling through the desert, we Christians are on our way to the heavenly Canaan. Our Father has fulfilled all the conditions necessary to prepare us for the imminent return of Jesus Christ.

"Eye hath not seen, nor ear heard, neither have entered into the heart of man, the things which God hath prepared for them that love him" (1 Cor. 2:9). The next verse in Corinthians tells us that these revelations are the work of the Holy Spirit (1 Cor. 2:10). Chapter 21 of Revelation is an undeniable example of what God has in store. I have no doubt that all humans are unanimous in believing that our world is full of beautiful things. People who have enough money to travel around the world often express great satisfaction in the beauty they have seen in many of the places they have been able to visit. Yet, imagine for a moment that the Word of God tells us that all this means nothing if we compare it to the marvelous things that Jesus has prepared for His chosen ones. Thinking carefully, we should be eager not only to see this event come, but we should also be eager to begin following Jesus in the present in preparation for His return.

God's Use of the Image of the Bride and Groom

Jesus Christ told a man who came to visit Him, "If I have told you earthly things, and ye believe not, how shall ye believe, if I tell you of heavenly things?" (John 3:12). He said this because earthly things are matters that are already knowable to all. As an expert and wise teacher, Jesus used the image of marriage to express His love for the human family and to make His love understandable to us. He used the powerful images and stories that usually trigger emotions to help us understand the immensity of His love.

He presented Himself as a young man in love with a young girl he wants to marry at all costs. The young girl represents the group of believers who accept His covenant and obey His word (see Matt. 25:1–13; 22:1–14). Since Jesus wanted to marry his beloved at all costs, He was willing to make the ultimate sacrifice of His life to carry out the promised blessings for Him and His bride. These blessings are the product of the death and resurrection of Jesus Christ in the lives of Christians, including justification by His blood, redemption, the outpouring of the Holy Spirit, the baptism of the Holy Spirit, the work of the Holy Spirit, and the new birth.

So, why did Jesus specially choose the image of marriage to express His great love for all humans? It is because it helps us imagine the grand happiness a man experiences the day he marries his beloved. Through this image, Jesus Christ expresses "the joy that was set before Him" (Heb. 12:2) in ministering on earth to institute the church and establish His kingdom. And not only did He experience joy, but His friends, the disciples, exulted with joy also, as well as those whose needs He met. Answering a question about fasting, Jesus said, "Can the children of the bridechamber mourn, as long as the bridegroom is with them?" (Matt. 9:15).

In order to highlight their importance, we can say that the Lord has taken care to bless and sanctify some of His institutions, which He Himself created for the well-being of humankind to give us full emotional, mental, and spiritual fulfillment and to ensure the sustainability of the human race (see Gen. 2:1–3, 23, 24). In the nineteenth chapter of Matthew, Jesus Christ took up the thought of Genesis 2 and added, "What therefore God hath joined together, let not man put asunder" (Matt. 19:6b). He speaks of the sacrificial love of marriage as an indissoluble covenant in which both partners love each other for life, respect each other, and practice faithfulness, mutual help, tolerance, and patience. In every marriage ceremony, performed according to the divine principles, there is always a unique stamp of the Creator. Because the invitation to marriage may not return, it should not be missed. It is a formal occasion in which the happy couple and the guests rejoice. It is the celebration of love.

During Bible times, a wedding ceremony could last up to a full week before the husband could leave with his wife. In the parable of the guests in Matthew 22, Jesus told the story of a king preparing a feast for the marriage of his son. He sent his servants to invite people to the wedding. The king represented God the Father, and the son represented Jesus Christ Himself. The servants are the prophets and the disciples, and the bride-to-be is the church preparing for the day of the wedding so that the church may present itself in unfailing beauty. The guests represent the people who have not yet sealed their covenant with Jesus Christ. In the parable of the ten young girls of Matthew 25, Jesus is presented as the groom. He promises that after the wedding, His wife will have a life of perfect and endless happiness in which "God shall wipe away all tears from their eyes; and there shall be no more death, neither sorrow, nor crying, neither shall there be any more pain: for the former things are passed away" (Rev. 21:4). Jesus told His disciples, "In my Father's house are many mansions: if it were not so, I would have told you. I go to prepare a place for you. And if I go and prepare a place for you, I will come again, and receive you unto myself; that where I am, there ye may be also" (John 14:2, 3).

The Power of Agapē Love

True love—*agapē* love—is expressed by a healthy attachment to and a high esteem for someone. We can call it "Christian love." It is a love that comes from God. The natural man cannot possess it. Yet, the Holy Spirit communicates it to the believer through the work of the new birth. In Romans 5:5, Paul emphasized that it is the work of the Holy Spirit to implant this love in the heart of the believer, and I would add that this is accomplished through a gradual process. At one time or another, most Christians have pondered why certain people, who are not practicing Christians, have a sincere love for their fellow men. Paul responds:

> "For merely listening to the law doesn't make us right with God. It is obeying the law that makes us right in his sight. Even Gentiles, who do not have God's written law, show that they know his law when they instinctively obey it, even without having heard it. They demonstrate that God's law is written in their hearts, for their own conscience and thoughts either accuse them or tell them they are doing right. And this is the message I proclaim—that the day is coming when God, through Christ Jesus, will judge everyone's secret life" (Rom. 2:13–16, NLT).

The power of *agapē* love is extreme. It exceeds all weapons of destruction. It effectively combats hatred, injustice, and all the bad traits of character that ravage humankind and that tarnish the image of the Creator in human beings. It is this love that motivated Jesus to come and die for all sinners without distinction—even when His creatures slapped Him and spit in His face, even when they condemned Him to die on the cross after a parody of a trial. He did not shrink from their verdict to disarm Satan and save humankind. The apostle Paul, who before his conversion to Christianity was a persecutor of Christians, said: "the love of Christ constraineth us" (2 Cor. 5:14). Yes, love engenders love. It is difficult not to respond in love to a person who loves so much (see John 17:26). Understanding how great God's love for us is, we are compelled by that love to love Him in return (2 Cor. 5:14). Out of love for humanity, Jesus was willing to experience humiliation. Through *agapē* love, Jesus was able to overcome insults of all kinds without thinking of revenge or availing Himself of His rights as our Creator.

How to Acquire Agapē Love

The natural man, which is a nature that comes from Adam, is carnal because "that which is born of the flesh is flesh" (John 3:6a). However, if people undergo the new birth, thanks to their collaboration with the interventions of the Holy Spirit, divine love can develop within, enabling them to live according to the Spirit. "That which is born of the Spirit is spirit" (John 3:6b). We have already mentioned that, under certain conditions, it is the work of the Holy Spirit to stir up love within us. Among other things, believers must make their personal decision to commit themselves with sincerity, in one way or another, to the service of the Lord. It is at this moment of decision that they give permission to the Holy Spirit through the commitment of baptism to intervene in their life, as their commitment was made in the name of the Father, the Son, and the Holy Spirit. It was to the Holy Spirit working in His disciples, that, by His word, Christ gave the responsibility of completing the work that He had begun.

An example of the fitting of the Spirit is seen in Gideon's choosing of the members of his army, when the great majority of men did not want to be there (Judges 7). This is why the Lord did not want Gideon to use them and why He commanded Gideon to dismiss those who really did not want to battle the enemy. These men were disqualified from taking up weapons in God's army. Their experience is a commentary on the spiritual reality of Christian life, for Paul compared believers to soldiers possessing spiritual weapons (see Eph. 6). Soldiers obey the orders of their hierarchical superiors. Their obedience, bravery, loyalty, discipline, and intelligence in making the right choice contribute to their promotion to greater responsibility. Through total commitment, they will develop a relationship of trust among their fellow soldiers.

"And I say unto you, Ask, and it shall be given you; seek, and ye shall find; knock, and it shall be opened unto you. For every one that asketh receiveth; and he that seeketh findeth; and to him that knocketh it shall be opened" (Luke 11:9, 10). The believer's search for divine blessings is progressive. We must search while continuing to ask. If our search does not produce the desired result, we must not hesitate to knock. God does not give greater blessings to those who remain inactive without risking anything. Of this truth the parable of the talents in Matthew 25 is a convincing example. The last of three servants, who had received a talent from the master, hid it until the master returned, explaining that he did so because he knew the master to be a hard man. Receiving no return on his investment with the servant, the master took the talent from that man and gave it to the first of the servants who had already proven himself capable of greater responsibility. Investing of our talents belongs to the realm of faith.

At the wedding of Cana, Jesus said to the servants, "Fill the jars with water" (John 2:7, ESV). When the organizer of the reception tasted the water, it had turned into wine—delicious wine! The servants had risked obedience and faith, bringing water not yet wine to the guests.

Another amazing story of faith is in Joshua 3. The river Jordan would be divided as was the Red Sea during the exodus of the Jewish people from Egypt. Yet, it must be noted that it was only when the priests who carried the ark of the Lord's covenant placed their feet in the water of the Jordan that the river was cut off upstream and stopped in a single mass. God chose not to manifest His power until the priests stepped, by faith, into the water (see Exod. 14:15, 16; Josh. 3:13–16). Often miracles have not occurred because we have been afraid to take a risk. Passive Christians who do not want to engage themselves cannot experience divine power. If we are inactive, the Holy Spirit cannot accomplish His work in us effectively.

To Love is the Essential Thing

"God is love; and he that dwelleth in love dwelleth in God, and God in him" (1 John 4:16).

> *The most important thing is to love, for the spiritual health of our heart determines our attitude toward God and our fellow men.*

The most important thing is to love, for the spiritual health of our heart determines our attitude toward God and our fellow men. When love is lacking, the heart can suffer from spiritual diseases such as pride, hypocrisy, and animosity, among other things. If the heart is sick, it will produce the fruit of its illness. Nonetheless, if it is healthy, it will produce the fruit of an optimal state of health. As we talk more about this later, it will help us to better understand why God promised to change the "heart" in Ezekiel 36:26, 27. This will require a review of Scripture to explain what the believer's heart represents for God.

Our Creator wants our love to reflect His love. For this to be so requires that we strive to mold our way of loving after His. All who aspire to be citizens of the kingdom of heaven must seek with eagerness to practice *agapē* love. Jesus has seen fit to give this mandate as a new commandment: "A new commandment I give unto you, That ye love one another; as I have loved you, that ye also love one another. By this shall all men know that ye are my disciples, if ye have love one to another" (John 13:34, 35). In answer to a question from the Pharisees, the Lord Jesus summarized the Ten Commandments of Exodus 20 in two. "Jesus said unto him, Thou shalt love the Lord thy God with all thy heart, and with all thy soul, and with all thy mind. This is the first and great commandment. And the second is like unto it, Thou shalt love thy neighbour as thyself. On these two commandments hang all the law and the prophets" (Matt. 22:37–40). If you return love for hatred, you may end up winning hostile hearts, though not always, for many will remain resistant despite the evidence of your love. That some resist should not keep you from loving. Nevertheless, according to the divine prescription, one day or another, you will reap your reward. "And let us not grow weary of doing good, for in due season we will reap, if we do not give up" (Gal. 6:9, ESV). Though it may be an arduous struggle that it is not always crowned with success, if you continue on to "overcome evil with good," you will glorify God and avoid giving the advantage to the enemy (Rom. 12:21). To continue loving, it is necessary to overlook difficulties, whatever their nature. It takes time to recover from some situations. Yet, it is imperative that we stay the course of *agapē* love.

The incomparable thirteenth chapter of the first Epistle to the Corinthians explains that *agapē* love matters most. To understand this masterpiece of the apostle Paul, defining the extreme importance of love, we must consider the two chapters that surround it. They imply that many Corinthian Christians were more attracted to some gifts than others. Some gifts such as the gift of prophecy and of speaking another language were more enviable than the others, and the enthusiasm for these gifts had created an unhealthy atmosphere among the believers.

The apostle began chapter 12 of First Corinthians by giving the criteria that distinguishes the Holy Spirit from evil spirits: "Wherefore I give you to understand, that no man speaking by the Spirit of God calleth Jesus accursed: and that no man can say that Jesus is the Lord, but by the Holy Ghost" (1 Cor. 12:3). By this he simply means that someone who is animated by an evil spirit cannot confess that Jesus Christ is Lord. A little farther on, in verses 22 to 24, Paul made it clear that "On the contrary, the parts of the body that seem to be weaker are indispensable, and on those parts of the body that we think less honorable we bestow the greater honor, and our unpresentable parts are treated with greater modesty, which our more presentable parts do not require. But God has so composed the body, giving greater honor to the part that lacked it" (1 Cor. 12:22–24, ESV). Addressing the Corinthians, he invites us not to be jealous of members who have received more visible gifts because, whatever the gift, it is important for the proper functioning of the body. The intervention of the apostle is to curtail the jealousy and envy between members of the body of Christ. To this end, he stressed the need for Christians to be inspired, without pretense, by genuine love from the Holy Spirit. Indeed, our words and our actions are often the fruit of our love. The words he uses are strong; the images are striking. No doubt, Paul wanted to spotlight the fact that love must be the trademark—the very essence—of Christian motivation. "But covet earnestly the best gifts: and yet shew I unto you a more excellent way" (1 Cor. 12:31). The more excellent way is that of *agapē*, which surpasses all other gifts. The following is the apostle's argument for the superiority of love in his message to the Christians of Corinth and to us today.

> *No doubt, Paul wanted to spotlight the fact that love must be the trademark—the very essence—of Christian motivation.*

If I speak in the tongues of men and of angels, but have not love, I am a noisy gong or a clanging cymbal. And if I have prophetic powers, and understand all mysteries and all knowledge, and if I have all faith, so as to remove mountains, but have not love, I am nothing. If I give away all I have, and if I deliver up my body to be burned, but have not love, I gain nothing. Love is patient and kind; love does not envy or boast; it is not arrogant or rude. It does not insist on its own way; it is not irritable or resentful; it does not rejoice at wrongdoing, but rejoices with the truth. Love bears all things, believes all things, hopes all things, endures all things. Love never ends. As for prophecies, they will pass away; as for tongues, they will cease; as for knowledge, it will pass away. For we know in part and we prophesy in part, but when the perfect comes, the partial will pass away. When I was a child, I spoke like a child, I thought like a child, I reasoned like a child. When I became a man, I gave up childish ways. For now we see in a mirror dimly, but then face to face. Now I know in part; then

I shall know fully, even as I have been fully known. So now faith, hope, and love abide, these three; but the greatest of these is love. (1 Cor. 13:1–13, ESV)

People had coveted the gifts that were apparently the most noticeable. However, Paul's message is that love surpasses all other gifts. He who does not possess love is like a resonating cymbal, a lightweight in the balances of the Lord. Peter Kreeft wrote that, according to St. John of the Cross, "At the twilight of our lives, we will be judged on how we have loved" (*The God Who Loves You*, chapter 6). We can conclude that *agapē* love is the pivot on which our Christian life must turn, and the quality of our love is the basis of our behavior towards our Creator and towards our neighbor.

The love of which we speak here is not the love of a friend, drawn from the Greek word *philia*. Nor is it love that relates to sexuality, which comes from the Greek *eros*. It is the great *agapē* love, which surpasses all and resists hostility, disdain, insult, injustice, and hatred. It is a disinterested, benevolent love that God communicates to us to help us transcend our own interests and triviality.

It is important to avoid falling into the trap of fanatical and superficial love adopted by those who think that Christians have the right to an easy life without difficulty. The sacred writings declare that a father chastises the child that he loves (Prov. 3:12). Parents who approve all the decisions of their child—good and bad—will receive, sooner or later, the reproaches of their child. We ask our children to dress appropriately to go to school and put down their electronic gadgets to give a little respite to their eyes. That they may not like our recommendations has nothing to do with whether we love them. On the contrary, we make these recommendations out of concern for their well-being (see Heb. 12:1–11). It is not well that we neglect messages about Christian edification and transformation and only deliver messages about love and grace. In bread, both the crust and the inside of the bread are fit for consumption. They come from the same dough, even though the crust can be a little harder to chew. So it is with the Word of God. It expresses the immeasurable love of God, yet it also contains laws to be observed, restrictions upon our human will, and reproof when we miss the mark (2 Tim. 3:16, 17).

Chapter 2

The Word of God is Powerful

The Word of God reflects God's personality and character. Without His Word, we would have a very vague idea of His person, His love, His work, and His plan of love for humanity. Jesus, the personified Word (John 1), gives us an insight into His pre-existence. His self reference, which He made in conversing with the Jews, emphasizes His superiority and pre-existence: "Verily, verily, I say unto you, Before Abraham was, *I am*" (John 8:58, emphasis added).

The Power of God's Word

We have often been intrigued by the power that is revealed in God's word. We have noticed in the Old Testament, as well as in the New Testament, all the wonders that the word of God has produced. According to His own will, He has lent His word to men to accomplish deeds. Throughout the first chapter of Genesis, the phrase "God said" is repeated in verse after verse (verses 1, 6, 9, 11, 14, 20, 24, 26, 28, 29). Each time that God speaks, what He expresses comes into existence.

In chapter 2, "the LORD God commanded the man, saying, Of every tree of the garden thou mayest freely eat: But of the tree of the knowledge of good and evil, thou shalt not eat of it: for in the day that thou eatest thereof thou shalt surely die" (Gen. 2:16, 17). In the next chapter, the man and his wife chose to disobey God's command as they ate of the forbidden tree. After their sin, God pronounced a sentence for the sin of each entity involved—for the serpent, for the woman, and for the man (Gen. 3:14–17). These divine words were executed to the letter. We experience and see their effects daily.

In Exodus, chapter 3, the Lord commanded Moses to tell the people Israel, who were enslaved in Egypt: "I AM hath sent me unto you" (Exod. 3:14). In the following chapter, as Moses complained of his difficulties in speech, the Lord reassured him with the words: "And the LORD said unto him, Who hath made man's mouth? or who maketh the dumb, or deaf, or the seeing, or the blind? have not I the LORD? Now therefore go, and I will be with thy mouth, and teach thee what thou shalt say" (Exod. 4:11). In this statement, God uses the imperfect verb "to be" (Heb. *hayah*), translated "I am," as His name. This would mean that He exists in His actions by the exploits that He was going to accomplish in Egypt in the eyes of the entire world through the intervention of Moses. He was made visible through His wonders, even if Pharaoh could not see Him physically.

The Bible only describes two things that God made with His hands—the Ten Commandments and man. He created all the other elements of the universe by His preferred method—His word. His word is active; it is powerful in rendering service to the Creator.

The Lord declares: "For as the rain cometh down, and the snow from heaven, and returneth not thither, but watereth the earth, and maketh it bring forth and bud, that it may give seed to the sower, and bread to the eater: So shall *my word* be that goeth forth out of my mouth: it shall not return unto me void, but it shall accomplish that which I please, and it shall prosper in the thing whereto I sent it" (Isa. 55:10, 11, emphasis added). Other servants besides Moses have been invested with the power of God's word. These include Elijah, Elisha, and all the other prophets, as well as the true Christians throughout the centuries. "Is not

> *The Bible only describes two things that God made with His hands—the Ten Commandments and man.*

my word like as a fire? saith the LORD; and like a hammer that breaketh the rock in pieces?" (Jer. 23:29, emphasis added).

The Greek word *rhēma* means that which is spoken, either verbally or in writing (Matt. 12:36). In short, it means a "word," but it can refer to a statement, instruction, or a speech. It also refers to the gospel, or to a word in the intellectual sense. Thus, speech (or *rhēma*) connects with human intelligence, as opposed to *logos*, which refers to divine thought and the expression of God's thought and will. *Logos* expresses a concept or an idea (Luke 7:7). *Logos* can also signify the word of the Lord or His revealed will about a direct revelation given by Christ (1 Thess. 4:15). It can also be a divine word spoken with authority and delivering supernatural power (Acts 10:36).

Jesus said: "The words that I speak unto you, they are spirit, and they are life" (John 6:63). Though His will is expressed in words, it is more than words. Above all, it is power in action. In 2 Timothy 3:16, the concept of divine inspiration in the sentence, "All scripture is inspired by God" (NASB), is translated from the Greek word *theopneustos*. This word is composed of two words: *Theos*, which means "God," and *pneo*, which means "to breathe," that is to say, "God breathed," or the "breath of God." This means that the word of God acts in symbiosis with the Holy Spirit. It is important to understand that God desires the application of His word—He wants His word to be put into practice in spite of Satan's fierce and constant opposition.

When the word of the Lord came to Jeremiah, the Lord God reassured him by showing him a branch of an almond tree (Heb. *shaqed*), which makes a play on words with the Hebrew verb *shaqad*, which means "to watch," or "to awaken" (translated "hasten" in Jer. 1:12).

Further on in the revelation of the plan of salvation, the apostle John personifies the word of God as the One who "was made flesh" (John 1:14). The apostle John, who came into privileged connection with Jesus Christ as His disciple, astonishes us in the first verses of his Gospel: "In the beginning was the Word [*logos*], and the Word was with God, and the Word was God. The same was in the beginning with God. All things were made by him; and without him was not any thing made that was made. In him was life; and the life was the light of men. And the light shineth in darkness; and the darkness comprehended it not" (John 1:1–5). In this statement, the beloved apostle steps foot into another dimension—the "word" He is describing is Jesus Christ Himself. If you have not yet experienced the power that comes through the name and blood of Jesus, it will benefit you to try them in various situations of life. Whether day or night, employ the name and blood of Jesus when you are in need of rescue, counsel, or anything else.

God uses the power of His word to save us. Paul said that the gospel is power for the salvation of anyone who believes (Rom. 1:16). Jesus Christ used God's word—the words of Scripture—to repel Satan at the moment of temptation (Matt. 4:4, 7, 10). His experience demonstrates why we need this powerful weapon in our possession at all times to deal with the suggestions of evil spirits that direct us to make bad decisions. When Jesus had sent out the seventy disciples, they returned joyfully with this report: "Lord, even the devils are subject unto us through thy name" (Luke 10:17).

God's goal is to integrate His word in us, to transform us, and to influence our behavior and actions. This is the meaning of the new covenant, in which God promises to inscribe His law in our hearts and minds. "This is the covenant that I will make with them after those days, saith the Lord, I will put my laws in their hearts, and in their minds will I write them" (Heb. 10:16). The power of speech is that it can transform those who apply it. We must ingest God's word so our very nature becomes saturated with it. According to Paul, it can separate our spirit from the hindrance of our soul, which is to say that it can contribute to the new birth (Heb. 4:12). God's word is a weapon that He has placed at our disposal to fight evil and evil's author. Presently, the word of God is everywhere, and is quite affordable. If need be, we can easily purchase a Bible for very little from a used bookstore. Despite its accessibility, the Bible is often abandoned and neglected. One rarely suspects all the divine power that is hidden in the word of God recorded in Scripture. Yet, it has transformed thousands of lives and is a safeguard for suicidal souls, a tutor for orphans, and a reliable educator against delinquency. It can also support the doctor's work in the healing of those who are sick. Whatever the state of your soul, whatever may be your past, the word of God can be your ultimate rehabilitative instrument.

Hebrews says: "For the word of God is living and active, sharper than any two-edged sword, piercing to the division of soul and of spirit, of joints and of marrow, and discerning the thoughts and intentions of the heart. And no creature is hidden from his sight, but all are naked and exposed to the eyes of him to whom we must give account" (Heb. 4:12, 13, ESV). How is it that the word of God can separate our "soul" from our "spirit," or mind? Our "soul" (Hebrew *nephesh;* Greek *psuchē*) represents our will. It is the seat of emotions and feelings (Luke 1:46). The term also refers to the natural life in us (Acts 20:10; Gen. 2:7). On the other hand, the "spirit," or mind, is the seat of human intelligence and morals—a person's consciousness and conscience (Luke 8:55). The spirit, or mind, allows us to think and reason, to make judicious choices. Our feelings introduce us to the vast field of emotions, which can be either good or bad. The apostle Peter, like the apostle Paul, exhorted the faithful to have "one mind" among them (1 Peter 3:8; 2 Cor. 13:11; Acts 17:11). Our emotions can be expressed in pride, joy, anger, kindness, hate, compassion, anxiety, sadness, enthusiasm, exultation, grief, etc. Emotions can lead us to God, but they can also move us away from Him. How can bad or undesirable emotions be eliminated? The answer is found in the death of the "old man" (Romans 6:6; 7:4). May the Holy Spirit who accompanies the word of God allow His word to produce its transformative work in your life and mine, for our spiritual growth!

Jesus Defined His Mission

After Jesus defeated Satan in the wilderness, he went back home to Nazareth.

> And Jesus returned in the power of the Spirit into Galilee: and there went out a fame of him through all the region round about. And he taught in their synagogues, being glorified of all. And he came to Nazareth, where he had been brought up: and, as his custom was, he went into the synagogue on the sabbath day, and stood up for to read. And there was delivered unto him the book of the prophet Esaias. And when he had opened the book, he found the place where it was written, The Spirit of the Lord is upon me, because he hath anointed me to preach the gospel to the poor; he hath sent me to heal the brokenhearted, to preach deliverance to the captives, and recovering of sight to the blind, to set at liberty them that are bruised, to preach the acceptable year of the Lord. And he closed the book, and he gave it again to the minister, and sat down. And the eyes of all them that were in the synagogue were fastened on him. And he began to say unto them, This day is this scripture fulfilled in your ears. (Luke 4:14–21)

On that Sabbath, Jesus did a unique thing in announcing Himself the fulfillment of Isaiah's prophecy. The passage that He quoted proved the truth of the word of God and set out His mission to heal psychological and physical wounds, free spiritual slaves, give sight to the spiritually blind, and preach the good news. Jesus passed this same mission on to His disciples.

The passage goes on, as Jesus "came down to Capernaum, a city of Galilee, and taught them on the sabbath days. And they were astonished at his doctrine: for his word was with power" (Luke 4:31, 32). In other words, Jesus spoke with authority.

> And there was in their synagogue a man with an unclean spirit; and he cried out, Let us alone; what have we to do with thee, thou Jesus of Nazareth? art thou come to destroy us? I know thee who thou art, the Holy One of God. And Jesus rebuked him, saying, Hold thy peace, and come out of him. And when the unclean spirit had torn him, and cried with a loud voice, he came out of him. And they were all amazed, insomuch that they questioned among themselves, saying, What thing is this? what new doctrine is this? for with authority commandeth he even the unclean spirits, and they do obey him. (Mark 1:21–27)

This story not only shows us the power of the word of Jesus Christ, it also reveals a certain reality of the invisible world. The devil, who is generally invisible to human perception, sees all that is taking place in the visible world. Unlike humans, he easily recognized the identity of Jesus Christ and took control of the man. He silenced the man's own thoughts and spoke in his place. Though since that incident the enemy has refined his techniques, even today he manifests himself in humanity. Notwithstanding the evidence of these facts written for our instruction, some believers have difficulty accepting and perceiving this spiritual reality.

Jesus Gives Us Power of Attorney in His Name

"Wherefore God also hath highly exalted him, and given him a name which is above every name: that at the name of Jesus every knee should bow, of things in heaven, and things in earth, and things under the earth; and that every tongue should confess that Jesus Christ is Lord, to the glory of God the Father" (Phil. 2:9–11). It is a great comfort and assurance for us to know that Jesus, who is our great Elder Brother, has all power in heaven, on earth, and under the earth. That is to say, He has power over the enemy and his army. He also has authority over sickness and death. He said to His disciples, "All authority in heaven and on earth has been given to me. Therefore go and make disciples of all nations, baptizing them in the name of the Father and of the Son and of the Holy Spirit, and teaching them to obey everything I have commanded you. And surely I am with you always, to the very end of the age" (Matt. 28:18–20, NIV). To this He added: "I give unto you power to tread on serpents and scorpions, and over all the power of the enemy: and nothing shall by any means hurt you" (Luke 10:19). We should emphasize that it is not without reason that Jesus called attention to these creatures, for evil spirits may, on occasion, borrow these creatures' forms, as was the case with the serpent in the Garden of Eden.

From the first chapter of the first book of the Bible, the Lord had already given man authority over all "creeping things" (the reptiles and insects that crawl on the earth). Jesus' statement is a reiteration of the authority that sin weakened but that still exists, according to the quality of each person's spiritual life. We must constantly remind ourselves that the reason Jesus asks us to remain in Him is so that we can use His name effectively. This does not mean only being a church member but also means remaining attached to Him in a close relationship by leading an active Christian life. As such, the branch bears fruit that comes from the vine because it shares the life of the vine. When a branch is attached to the vine, it cannot be easily detached. To sever the branch, one must use great force or a mechanical or electrical tool, such as a saw. Branches can also be severed by storms and cyclones. However, as much as it depends on our will, we have an obligation to remain attached. If we express the desire to stay connected, Jesus will come to make it so.

Our concern should be to cooperate with the Spirit of God in His work of transformation in us that He may endow us with His spiritual weapons. We may even be surprised to see that non-believers in Jesus have used His name, under certain circumstances, to escape from a dangerous situation.

Jesus Christ received a new title after His ascension—He is Lord—according to the order of our heavenly Father. The universal and unlimited power of His name is our assurance in the struggle against evil and its author. It is a great privilege for us to use the power hidden in the name of Jesus as a formidable weapon to defend ourselves and repel Satan and his army.

Our Lord has all authority in heaven and on earth and under the earth to delegate to His servants, within the framework of His will, the power to act in His name. He is also our great Elder Brother, our Redeemer, and our Righteousness. He also gives us access to God who becomes our Father again through our rebirth as His child. He promised to be with all those who work to advance the cause of His kingdom. He gives us power in the course of His work. He is present to support us in difficult situations and to defend us against the assaults of the enemy. For all this to be possible, we must be grafted into Jesus Christ and remain attached to Him that we may produce fruits through the grafting of the Holy Spirit. It is through the Holy Spirit that Jesus abides within us to ensure us of His infallible support.

Jesus gave power to His disciples for all times, though certain implicit conditions apply. Before considering someone a friend and giving him power of attorney for important transactions, we want to be sure that our friend is worthy of such confidence. It is the same for Jesus Christ. He invites us to remain attached to Him as branches of the vine that we may produce fruit worthy of our Creator.

Jesus' Focus on Essential Things

In general, a good teacher takes care to emphasize, in a class presentation, subjects that are likely to be part of the course's final examination. This is done to encourage students to thoroughly assimilate class presentations so they can pass the final exam from the training received during their studies. The expression "in truth," which comes from the Greek word *amēn*, is a word borrowed from the Hebrew. It means "really" or "definitely." Jesus used it in many situations to reinforce the truth of His declarations and the certainty of what His declarations would accomplish.

He uses *amēn*, translated "verily" in Matthew 5:18, in speaking about the law. He speaks of rewards for our wise choices and of consequences for disregarding His word (Matt. 5:26; 24:47; Mark 9:41; Luke 12:37). Jesus promised a woman, who anointed His head with perfume, that her benevolent action would be immortalized with the retelling of the gospel story (Matt. 26:13). He talked about the future of the kingdom of God, about tax collectors and prostitutes who are sincerely repentant (Matt. 21:31), and about the certainty of what His disciples bind on earth being bound in heaven (Matt. 18:18).

Now the Savior turns a corner. "Then said Jesus unto his disciples, Verily I say unto you, That a rich man shall hardly enter into the kingdom of heaven" (Matt. 19:23). Here Jesus no doubt wanted to focus on the problems that come with wealth. Wealth makes life easy; it confers a certain power and privilege to those who have it over other people. It may even have been gained through the exploitation of the most vulnerable. Wealth allows the possessor to have hangers on, often without wanting them. Indeed, imagine yourself with all the facilities that a rich person can have, sometimes without much effort. You can buy goods to create an idyllic environment with services of all kinds. One might think that such a life would be so easy that it would be like living on a cloud, in a world apart. However, the downside is that the many hangers on will attract us to slippery slopes or that pleasures will come knocking at our door. We could draw up a more exhaustive list of the possible benefits and disadvantages that often litter the pathway of the rich, to demonstrate how good and evil can intertwine in a person's life. Yet, I hope that these brief ideas have inspired you and that they have given you a more accurate description of the perils in the life of the wealthy.

Jesus passes to the other end of the spectrum, pronouncing judgment on the selfish: "For I was an hungered, and ye gave me no meat: I was thirsty, and ye gave me no drink: I was a stranger, and ye took me not in: naked, and ye clothed me not: sick, and in prison, and ye visited me not. Then shall they also answer him, saying, Lord, when saw we thee an hungered, or athirst, or a stranger, or naked, or sick, or in prison, and did not minister unto thee? Then shall he answer them, saying, Verily I say unto you, Inasmuch as ye did it not to one of the least of these, ye did it not to me" (Matt. 25:42–45). We can see in this text that Jesus speaks of the hungry, the thirsty, the immigrant, the traveler, the needy, the sick, and the imprisoned. It is a wide range of people who are vulnerable because of their economic, social, or geographic state. History shows that these people represent groups that are more likely to accept the grace and salvation offered by the Lord. A traveler could remain comfortably at his home, but, as a stranger in a foreign country, he needs help. To respond to Jesus' recommendation, we must be filled with *agapē* love. Jesus has kind regard for all who make sacrifices to follow Him.

"And Jesus answered and said, Verily I say unto you, There is no man that hath left house, or brethren, or sisters, or father, or mother, or wife, or children, or lands, for my sake, and the gospel's, but he shall receive an hundredfold now in this time, houses, and brethren, and sisters, and mothers, and children, and lands, with persecutions; and in the world to come eternal life" (Mark 10:29, 30). Jesus assures us that He will take care of us if we choose to serve Him under precarious situations. He will provide for all our material needs. He promises to multiply by a hundred what we have abandoned, in addition to granting us eternal life. These promises reassure us of His unwavering support even under circumstances that may seem desperate in our eyes.

Jesus also addressed Nicodemus on a subject of vital importance to spiritual life: "Verily, verily, I say unto thee, Except a man be born again, he cannot see the kingdom of God. Nicodemus saith unto him, How can a man be born when he is old? can he enter the second time into his mother's womb, and be born? Jesus answered, Verily, verily, I say unto thee, Except a man be born of water and of the Spirit, he cannot enter into the kingdom of God. That which is born of the flesh is flesh; and that which is born of the Spirit is spirit. " (John 3:3–6).

> *We have the duty to struggle to the point of gaining the upper hand with sin by the power of the Holy Spirit.*

Jesus also talked about the importance of not engaging in sin. We have the duty to struggle to the point of gaining the upper hand with sin by the power of the Holy Spirit. "Verily, verily, I say unto you," Jesus said, "Whosoever committeth sin is the servant of sin" (John 8:34). The purpose of the Lord is not merely to forgive us but to break the power of sin in us. It is the role of the death of the carnal man and of the presence of the Holy Spirit who is the life of Jesus in us. Paul calls attention to those who have "resisted unto blood, striving against sin" (Heb. 12:4). Though Paul did not precede his declarations with "verily, verily," he did use a style of writing, familiar to his early readers, that would convince them of the veracity and importance of the messages he delivered.

Jesus said: "Ye call me Master and Lord: and ye say well; for so I am. If I then, your Lord and Master, have washed your feet; ye also ought to wash one another's feet. For I have given you an example, that ye should do as I have done to you. Verily, verily, I say unto you, The servant is not greater than his lord; neither he that is sent greater than he that sent him. If ye know these things, happy are ye if ye do them" (John 13:13–17). In this text, the Lord Jesus touched a very important point for our daily Christian life. In the Semeur Study Bible, a very pertinent comment is made. In ancient times, shoes did not protect the feet from dirt, dust, and the excrement of animals strewn in the streets. After walking some distance, the feet were coated with a mixture of these unhealthy elements because animals were the main means of transportation on land. After walking in the filthy streets, it was customary, for the sake of hygiene, for a person to wash his or her feet or, at least, to have them washed by a servant. On the night He was betrayed, Jesus Christ told Peter that, if he did not allow Him to wash his feet, he would not gain access to Christ's kingdom. Thus we witness Jesus practicing and recommending this social courtesy as a symbol of humility and mutual forgiveness between believers, which must be practiced in daily relationships in order to maintain Christian harmony in the image of the body of Christ. The dirt that sticks to the feet of travelers compares to the small indiscretions that could be the flash point of conflict between believers. Because of the importance of this recommendation, Jesus associated it with a spiritual blessing: that those who understand and implement His exhortation will be happy. It is important to focus our attention on these essential texts, which contain beneficial messages for the Christian journey. Jesus' declarations, which are preceded or succeeded by the words "in truth," must not go unnoticed.

Jesus' Power over Sickness and Death

There is a power that can cure us of our psychological and physical illnesses. Before Jesus' first advent, sickness and death reigned supreme on the earth. Indeed, Jesus came to overthrow these conditions in which humankind was held prisoner of Satan. "When the even was come, they brought unto him many that were possessed with devils: and he cast out the spirits with his word, and healed all that were sick: that it might be fulfilled which was spoken by Esaias the prophet, saying, Himself took our infirmities, and bare our sicknesses" (Matt. 8:16, 17). From the moment that sin began to exercise its dominion over mankind, men and women have been spiritually imprisoned to the evil one, often without realizing it. In order to protect themselves from death, they associate themselves with the instigator of death. But this arrangement is like asking a rabbit to guard a carrot. He may resist the temptation to eat it for a while to give the impression that he is trustworthy. However, if he is hungry, he will not hesitate to eat the carrot placed under his guardianship because carrots are his favorite food. "Forasmuch then as the children are partakers of flesh and blood, he also himself likewise took part of the same; that through death he might destroy him that had the power of death, that is, the devil; and deliver them who through fear of death were all their lifetime subject to bondage" (Heb. 2:14, 15). This is wonderful news! Jesus Christ, our Savior, Lord and brother, recovers by His death and resurrection the keys of death and the abode of the dead, which were in the hands of Satan. This means that He has the power to give life and to enter into the abode of the dead. "I am he that liveth, and was dead; and, behold, I am alive for evermore, Amen; and have the keys of hell and of death" (Rev. 1:18). Only in Him can we find a sure refuge.

Jesus bore our curses to give us authority and victory over sickness and death. He holds the keys of death and the abode of the dead. Therefore, He said of the church, "The gates of hell [and of death, Rev. 1:18] shall not prevail against it" (Matt. 16:18). It remains for us to place our trust in Jesus, to enjoy His many blessings. Worry and fear cause us to lose our ability to overcome evil. Our thoughts often lead us to unreal paths in hopes of living an imaginary reality. They weaken our mental faculties, indispensable to nourish and solidify our faith. Norman Vincent Peale reported in his book "The Power of Positive Thinking" the story of a man who had a practically incurable bone tumor, according to his physician. This man was devastated after he became aware of his state of health. He frequented the church, although he was not particularly religious, he said. He rarely read the Bible. "One day," he reported, "as I lay in my bed, it occurred to me that I would like to read the Bible, and I asked my wife to bring me one. She was very surprised, for I have never before made such a request. I began to read, and found consolation and comfort." Then the more he read, the more he noticed his condition improving. One day, during Bible reading, he experienced a curious sensation of warmth and indescribable inner well-being. After this, his healing accelerated. As his improvement was evident, he saw his doctors who noted his recovery with amazement (*The Power of Positive Thinking*, pp. 179, 180). So he was healed by faith as he perseveringly read his Bible, the conduit of the power of God. The power of God is available to all who believe in Him. "And these signs shall follow them that believe; in my name shall they cast out devils; they shall speak with new tongues; they shall take up serpents; and if they drink any deadly thing, it shall not hurt them; they shall lay hands on the sick, and they shall recover" (Mark 16:17, 18). To perform

> *If we begin to convince ourselves that we are and always will be sinners and that Adam is our father, then it will be very difficult for us to acquire the new nature of Christ, which the Holy Spirit has the mission to implant progressively in us. In Romans 6:11, the apostle exhorts us.*

the Lord's work effectively, believers must be invested with the power of the Holy Spirit. They must also banish from their life all the behaviors that are likely to sadden the Holy Spirit and keep the Spirit apart from them.

By faith we can experience the demonstration of the promises of our Lord and Savior, Jesus Christ. When we believe that we have received the thing we have asked for, the Holy Spirit, in His power, begins to execute His will in us, and we shall see fulfilled that which we have requested (Mark 11:24). The Word of God tells us that we are children of God and joint-heirs with Christ (John 1:12; Rom. 8:17). Our role is to behave like children of God without listening to our first nature from Adam. When we pray to God to grant us the Holy Spirit so we can benefit from His work, we are to act by faith as children of God. Faith is a mental demonstration of the things we hope for. Doubt and denial can prevent the Holy Spirit from doing His transforming work in our lives. If we begin to convince ourselves that we are and always will be sinners and that Adam is our father, then it will be very difficult for us to acquire the new nature of Christ, which the Holy Spirit has the mission to implant progressively in us. In Romans 6:11, the apostle exhorts us: "… reckon ye also yourselves to be dead indeed unto sin." The sixth chapter of the epistle to the Ephesians presents the word of God as "the sword of the Spirit" (Eph. 6:17). Then we must trust in His word, the expression of His will, so that God will be able to fulfill His promises for us. The word of God is powerful (Heb. 4:12); the faith that we exhibit allows God to put His power into action. We have a great share of responsibility in determining whether or not the will of God is done on earth as it is in heaven.

Chapter 3
The Prophecies, a Divine Signature

Skeptics question the divine authorship of the Bible. However, there is one feature of Scripture that points, like no other, to Scriptures' divine authorship. It is the uncanny revelations of prophecy. As Daniel told the Babylonian king about his night vision: "There is a God in heaven that revealeth secrets, and maketh known to the king Nebuchadnezzar what shall be in the latter days" (Dan. 2:28).

Remarkable Prophecies in Daniel 2, 4, and 5

There is no one besides the Creator God who can predict the future under all circumstances with unfailing precision. No one but He knows the secrets of the heart of humankind. In Daniel 2, all the king's magicians and astrologers told him that it was impossible to know what he had seen in his dream, yet the Creator God easily revealed it to His servant Daniel. Examples such as these abound in the Bible, and our daily experiences also bear witness to God's foreknowledge. How many times has God warned us in anticipation of something that was going to happen in our lives? He knows everything that will happen in everyone's life—down to the smallest detail.

The prophecy of Daniel 2 explains the course of the history of the world from the year 605 BC until the return of Christ. The four parts of the statue correspond to the different kingdoms that we shall name below. We will indicate approximate dates for the prophecy of Daniel 2 to facilitate the understanding of readers who have a limited knowledge of the Bible. These dates may vary slightly depending on the notes in one's Bible. The Babylonian Empire reigned from about 605 BC to about 539 BC, at which time the empire of the Medes and Persians seized power from Babylon with King Cyrus as their head. Around 333 BC, Greece, under Alexander the Great, became the dominant empire. Around 63 BC, Rome came to power as the dominant world empire. The ministry of Jesus began with His baptism in AD 27. Following AD 30, Jesus' crucifixion and ascension to heaven, and Pentecost, the Christian church had its birth. It was Jesus who said, "…the kingdom of God is come unto you" (Matt. 12:28).

The fact that the various conquering countries, which correspond to the different parts of the giant statue, have succeeded each other as God indicated in the dream confirms the accuracy of God's foreknowledge and predictions.

This prophecy is remarkable because it covers a large part of the history of this world. Chapter 4 of Daniel presents the prophecy that King Nebuchadnezzar, who, because of his pride, would spend seven years in the wild living with the animals. Once again, this prophecy was fulfilled accurately. Nebuchadnezzar was driven from the midst of men to live with the wild beasts for a period of seven years. At the end of this period, he confessed the supremacy and authority of the Creator God, and his kingdom was restored to him. These events recorded in the Bible prove that it bears the signature of the Spirit of God. In the next chapter, we will come back to an important facet of the prophecy of Daniel chapter 2.

The Prophetic Accuracy of the Word of God

The plan of salvation has long been announced—ever since the fall of man. The Lord foretold this plan by killing a lamb so He could use its skin to cover the nakedness of Adam and Eve. Other prophetic declarations confirmed the will of God to restore man by the coming of a Savior. He promised to put hostility between the offspring of the woman and the offspring of Satan (Gen. 3:15). There are many prophecies in the Old Testament concerning the life, death, and resurrection of Jesus. The fulfillment of these prophecies is an evident demonstration of the power of the word of God and the coherent work of the Holy Spirit through the Bible. No human can predict the future with such accuracy, particularly when it is often given several centuries in advance of the events predicted. However, it is a mere formality for the Creator God.

There is a prediction in Isaiah 40:3 concerning John the Baptist. Its fulfillment is described in Matthew 3:1, 2. Another prophecy about Jesus was announced in Zechariah 9:9, and its fulfillment is found in Luke 19:35–37. A prophecy of Micah 5:2 is realized in Matthew 2:6. A prediction about Judah in Zechariah 11:12 is realized in Matthew 26:15. A pronouncement in Isaiah 53:9 is fulfilled in Matthew 27:57–60. And, last of all, the prophecy of Psalm 22:18 is fulfilled in John 19:23, 24. Despite the skepticism of some people, it is evident that the Bible is the work of the Holy Spirit and that it contains everything that is essential to lead us on the path of salvation and eternity.

The fulfillment of these prophecies is an evident demonstration of the power of the word of God and the coherent work of the Holy Spirit through the Bible.

God Limited the Human Lifetime by His Word

Then the LORD said: "My Spirit shall not abide in man forever, for he is flesh: his days shall be 120 years" (Gen. 6:3, ESV). The Semeur Study Bible translates this text thus: "My spirit will not fight indefinitely with men, because of their faults. They are beings dominated by their weaknesses. I give them another hundred and twenty years to live." There is one thing that is common between these two versions, God made His decision based on the carnality of humankind. We have two more questions to answer: First, is this "Spirit" the Holy Spirit or is it the spirit of man? Second, is the hundred and twenty years a time of grace that began at the time of this divine declaration until the flood, or did God want to limit the lifespan of a human to 120 years? We will consult the facts and try to answer these questions. In Genesis 5, verse 32, Noah is five hundred years old. In Genesis 6, starting with verse 8, God announced the flood. Genesis 7, verse 6, reports that Noah was six hundred years old at the time of the flood. In verse 11, Noah was still 600 years old during the flood. By the first day of the first month, the surface of the earth had dried, and Noah was 601 years old (Gen. 8:13). This means that 101 years passed from the announcement of the flood until it was over. So it would seem that the 120 years do not correspond to a time of grace culminating in the deluge.

Another possibility would be that the 120 years corresponds to the age limit a man can reach. After the creation, men lived a long time—in fact, compared to today, they lived a very long time. Methuselah lived 969 years (Gen. 5:27). Noah lived 950 years (Gen. 9:29). Terah, Abram's father, lived 250 years (Gen. 11:32). Sara, Abraham's wife, lived 127 years (Gen. 23:1). Abraham lived 175 years (Gen. 25:7). Ishmael lived 130 years (Gen. 25:17). Isaac lived 180 years (Gen. 35:28). Jacob lived 147 years (Gen. 47:28). Joseph lived 110 years (Gen. 50:22). From the time of God's declaration, which fixed the age of man at one hundred and twenty years, the human lifespan began to diminish and stabilize at around one hundred and twenty years. The diminishing of age limits, as seen above, lends plausibility to this being the proper interpretation of God's statement in Genesis 6:3.

The seventh verse of Ecclesiastes 12 agrees with the idea of the limit of the age of man. This text tells us: "Then shall the dust return to the earth as it was: and the spirit shall return unto God who gave it." This means that, at death, God takes back the spirit that He put in man. Moreover, the Old Testament does not say that the Lord gave the Holy Spirit to every person among His people. Rather, the Holy Spirit was only given to people entrusted with specific roles, such as kings, judges, and prophets. Only from Pentecost on did the Holy Spirit become available to all believers. Moreover, the state of depravity of humankind, as described in Genesis 6, implies that the Holy Spirit could not remain in him. It would seem reasonable that the text is alluding to the spirit *of man*, which returns to God at the moment of his death at the end of a lifespan fixed at around 120 years, though the Spirit of God is what sustains our life.

When God Speaks

This topic was not part of what I originally outlined to cover in this book. However, a circumstance arose compelling me to introduce it. I hope that you enjoy it. It is the result of an interview I had with an energetic and motivated Christian sister during the writing of the book. Probing what should be the normal life of a Christian, we will review some important statements recorded in the sacred Scriptures. When many signs of the return of Jesus Christ multiply and succeed each other, we believe that Christians are called to scrutinize their habits and practices in rela-

Chapter 3 *The Prophecies, a Divine Signature*

tion to the word of God. As believers, we recognize the impact of new and unusual things that have become a part of modern life. Opportunities for monitoring, control, and communications are unlimited due to the rapid development of digital and computer technology. Surprising news reports sometimes reveal debasing practices that further tarnish the image of the Creator in humankind. The question that always comes back to us is: What must we do, or what can we do more, to respond to the divine requirements as prescribed in God's Word?

We live in an era in which people tend to adapt spiritual requirements to a standard that ignores the real abilities of the spiritual nature that Christ has given us. While most Christians agree that the return of Jesus is near, it is still profitable that we reflect upon the reality of our Christian life and what it should be. The Bible—in particular Matthew 24—contains signs in the world that announce the return of Christ. A single glance around us is enough to show that we are almost at the finish line of the Christian race. The opposing team is ardently preparing for the final sprint. If, by chance, we started the race badly or are falling behind, it is time that we make every effort to catch up. In competing against a strong opponent, training is essential.

> *We live in an era in which people tend to adapt spiritual requirements to a standard that ignores the real abilities of the spiritual nature that Christ has given us.*

After Israel had spent more than four hundred years in Egypt, the Lord chose to deliver His people from slavery and lead them into Canaan through His chosen mediator, Moses. Nonetheless, after they had spent all that time in a foreign country, the Lord wanted the people to remain a few years in the wilderness—far from the influence of the surrounding pagan nations—to re-educate them according to His will before they could enter the Promised Land. Contrary to what one might have thought, it was a difficult experience for the people as well as it was for Moses, even though he "was very meek, above all the men which were upon the face of the earth" (Num. 12:3). Despite this fact, Moses disqualified himself from entering Canaan by disobeying God's direct command to "speak to the rock" (Num. 20:8) as he lost patience with the rebelliousness of the people. "And Moses lifted up his hand, and with his rod he smote the rock twice: and the water came out abundantly, and the congregation drank, and their beasts also. And the LORD spake unto Moses and Aaron, Because ye believed me not, to sanctify me in the eyes of the children of Israel, therefore ye shall not bring this congregation into the land which I have given them" (Num. 20:11, 12). Despite their error, the LORD did not forsake His servants. However, their angry response had irreversible consequences. With the noble task Moses was given of leading God's people, God rightfully held him to a high standard of behavior. Yet, from our modern Christian point of view, we would expect the LORD to react with greater leniency.

Since the first advent of Jesus Christ, we have lived under the reign of grace in God's spiritual kingdom, and we are waiting for Christ's second advent, which will establish God's kingdom on earth for all humankind. In modern times, the rule of law and liberty has gradually been established in most of the countries of the world. Imagine for a moment how our modern world would relate to Moses if he were to act now as he did on Sinai. He would be thrown into prison for striking the people with the two tables of stone after they made a feast to the golden calf (Exod. 32). With the people either dead or wounded, Moses would be sentenced for assault and murder. By our modern standard, we would judge Jesus as saying: Forgive the people and ask them to discontinue their idol worship. I imagine that the people under Moses lived in fear—the fear of being stoned for any violation of God's law. God is love as much as He is sovereign. At this point in the unfolding of the plan of salvation, God judges that we have arrived at a time in which free choice must take precedence over compunction and fear. Having been given a proper moral education, God gives us, His children, the freedom to make informed and responsible choices in relation to our previous education. Thus, His regime of grace gives us greater peace and freedom, and we rejoice in that freedom. Yet, such freedom also tests our motives and our ability to make the right choice. That is why Jesus invites us to enter voluntarily through the narrow entryway. "Enter by the narrow gate. For the gate is wide and the way is easy that leads to destruction, and those who enter by it are many. For the gate is narrow and the way is hard that leads to life, and those who find it are few" (Matt. 7:13, 14).

I have a 10-year-old son who likes watching certain television shows. He tends to neglect his school work when watching television. Since he is still a child, I, as his parent and tutor, am responsible for getting him back on task. As an adult, I am more disadvantaged than he is because I do not have a human tutor over me who intervenes directly with me to bring me back to order. If I love things that can harm my relationship with God, I am free to exercise my will to choose to engage in those things—to my detriment. We must remember that God loves us the same as He loved the people of Israel—He does not change. No one else in the Bible ever developed as close a relationship with God as did Moses or had such favor with God. His friendship with God was so intense that he wanted to see God's face. At least twice God changed His mind about judging His people because of Moses' intercession with Him. Nevertheless, after he made the mistake of striking the rock against God's directions, God did not indulge his actions or give him special treatment. He did not have another opportunity to recover. He missed the privilege of entering Canaan. Today, we may try to please everyone. Yet, we need to bow to the authority of the word of the Lord, which alone can satisfy.

After a certain time, when someone repeats an action enough, it becomes a habit, or second nature. If enough people do likewise, we might say, that is how it is done. If someone should complain, "That is not the way it used to be done," people will say the person is old-fashioned. To avoid the stigma of being considered different, most people conform. Conformity is merely a matter of convenience. Yet, each of us has a responsibility to seek to know the will of God. "And if a soul sin, and commit any of these things which are forbidden to be done by the commandments of the LORD; though he wist it not, yet is he guilty, and shall bear his iniquity" (Lev. 5:17). The Lord does not "grade on the curve." He will not lower the standard as a teacher might do for an examination to set the score for passing according to the average of the class. We must remember that Jesus Himself said, "But as the days of Noe were, so shall also the coming of the Son of man be" (Matt. 24:37). It is true that the world before the flood was not as crowded as it is today. Yet, when we consider that only eight people from a single family entered the ark, we can safely conclude that, in spiritual matters, truth is seldom found on the side of the majority. On the other hand, the fact that we have a more complete revelation of God's plan and expectations than did the people who lived in Old Testament times tells us that we will be judged differently—according to the education and revelation we have received. Jesus said: "Verily I say unto you, It shall be more tolerable for the land of Sodom and Gomorrha in the day of judgment, than for that city" (Matt. 10:15). He was speaking of any city that does not receive His disciples.

I remember a preacher who made the illuminating statement that truth always presents itself totally naked, that is to say, without a covering. Systematic study of the Bible aids in the spiritual development of believers, for it is an undeniable truth that there is power in the word of God. That power is released for all those who devote themselves to reading the Bible. The goal of every true Christian is to see Jesus Christ one day face to face and obtain the eternal crown. The Bible is a vast field of study encompassing plains, hills, mountains, valleys, rivers, steep inclines, and gradual slopes. It takes time for readers to apply themselves to the exploration of the Bible by the help of the Holy Spirit. If we do not do our own exploration, we will miss much of "the view" and be left with someone else's appraisal about the Bible—that it is only a large plain or a valley or a desert oasis.

From the first chapter of the Bible to the very last, God's love stands out. All Scripture demonstrates that God is love and that He loves His human children. Yet, we must also understand that His love for His children is not blind. What father who loves his child will let him fall into a hole without warning him that his path is dangerous. In Jeremiah 18:8–10, the Lord spoke to his people, saying, "If that nation, against whom I have pronounced, turn from their evil, I will repent of the evil that I thought to do unto them. And at what instant I shall speak concerning a kingdom, to build and to plant it; if it do evil in my sight, that it obey not my voice, then I will repent of the good, wherewith I said I would benefit them." Our attitude influences divine decisions about our future.

Jesus told the twelve disciples that He still had many things to teach them, which the promised Comforter would undertake to do (John 16:12, 13). This would mean that the disciples did not then have the maturity to assimilate these new teachings. It would also mean that the disciples then had an incomplete revelation. This implies that there would be other important revelations in the writings of the apostles after Jesus ascended to heaven. Therefore, the writings of the apostles deserve our full attention. (See also Heb. 12:4–8.)

Indeed, we recognize the unpopularity of certain texts that we use in this section since they reveal unavoidable truths concerning our salvation. Jesus loves us; these truths have the object of awakening our conscience. The word of God has the ability to disturb us and to correct us for the sake of our eternal life. The main purpose of the church is to lead us to Christ and reproduce the image of Christ in us that we might obtain the eternal crown. The social aspect of the human experience plays an important role in leading people to Christ and in fostering a sense of our corporate brotherhood. Yet, once a person embarks upon the path of the Lord, the spiritual aspect human experience needs to take over. I hope that what we have just covered has been for you an invitation to further reflection on the state of the Christian journey.

Chapter 4
The Divine Revelation

The Creator God reveals Himself to us through the Bible, written over several centuries under the inspiration of the Holy Spirit by authors living in different generations and endowed with various levels of education. Their unity of spirit comes from the fact that they were all in the school of the greatest teacher of the universe, the Holy Spirit. Some scriptures refine and confirm others, allowing God's revelation of truth to be more explicit. Thus, the answers to questions that arise in one part of the sacred writings can be found in another. The imprint of the Holy Spirit makes the Bible a book above all other books because its true author is God. From its very first pages, it is a divine revelation of the plan of salvation and restoration of humanity, which only becomes clearer throughout Scripture until the plan is realized in the Seed of the woman (Gen. 3:15). Of course, God is revealed in other ways.

In addition to all divine wonders and the various angelic appearances recorded in the Bible, the Creator God reveals Himself in nature through the complexity and precision of the laws that govern the universe. "For his invisible attributes, namely, his eternal power and divine nature, have been clearly perceived, ever since the creation of the world, in the things that have been made. So they are without excuse" (Rom. 1:20, ESV). God is revealed, in a general way, as the intelligent designer behind the complexity and perfection of human anatomy and physiology. He is also revealed by His various names in Scripture, which describe a particular aspect of His character. Above all, He is revealed by the biblical prophecies, through which He expresses His will for humankind and unfolds the plan of salvation for the preservation of the human race.

> *The imprint of the Holy Spirit makes the Bible a book above all other books because its true author is God.*

The Bible unfolds truth with a simplicity and a perfect adaptation to the needs and longings of the human heart, that has astonished and charmed the most highly cultivated minds, while it enables the humblest and uncultured to discern the way of salvation. And yet these simply stated truths lay hold upon subjects so elevated, so far-reaching, so infinitely beyond the power of human comprehension, that we can accept them only because God has declared them. Thus the plan of redemption is laid open to us, so that every soul may see the steps he is to take in repentance toward God and faith toward our Lord Jesus Christ, in order to be saved in God's appointed way; yet beneath these truths, so easily understood, lie mysteries that are the hiding of His glory—mysteries that overpower the mind in its research, yet inspire the sincere seeker for truth with reverence and faith. The more he searches the Bible, the deeper is his conviction that it is the word of the living God, and human reason bows before the majesty of divine revelation. (*Steps to Christ*, pp. 107, 108)

"God, who at sundry times and in divers manners spake in time past unto the fathers by the prophets, hath in these last days spoken unto us by his Son, whom he hath appointed heir of all things, by whom also he made the worlds" (Heb. 1:1, 2). These verses effectively report that God revealed Himself to His children many times and in various ways in the Old Testament but that His best revelation came through Jesus Christ. The implication of this is that the plan of redemption is not revealed all at once. Our heavenly Father presents His plan to us in a gradual way, in connection with our spiritual maturity and the light He has revealed to us.

Divine Revelation is a Gradual Process

After humankind descended into the depths of the abyss of sin, the Lord sought to rehabilitate His human children through simple and familiar methods of re-education. He used concrete images to prepare us to understand the more abstract realities of the plan of redemption. He not only revealed His existence in the form of a human and angels, but He has also worked through visible symbols to aid humans in discovering important facets of the plan of salvation.

In the Old Testament, God carried out His plan in specific situations through the Holy Spirit. Yet, God's Spirit often spoke through the "angel of the Lord" (e.g., Gen. 16:7–11; 22:11–15; Num. 22:22–35; Judges 2:1–4; 6:11–22; 13:3–21; etc.). Upon one fact we can all agree—an encounter with the angel of the Lord is an intense spiritual experience of unbelievable value. Those who have an encounter with God's messenger will never be the same, for they will advance several steps forward in the Christian journey. This is why these angelic appearances, which were a form of divine revelation, were so frequent in the Old Testament. Their aim was to transform, educate, and strengthen humans spiritually. In the same way that God, according to His sovereign election, chose the people of Israel, so did He also choose Moses to lead His people. It is important to note that God gave His chosen people, according to the Scriptures, the mission of making Him known to the other peoples of the earth. Thus, with the first advent of Jesus, the outpouring of the Holy Spirit, and the writings of the apostles, the unfolding of the plan of salvation, which leads us to eternal life, was complete.

It would seem that, early on, humankind did not have the ability to conform to the divine guidelines presented formally on Sinai, in spite of the repeated appearances of the angels of God and the manifestation of God's presence before the people. They never stopped violating God's guidelines—even when the covenant with their Creator had just been accepted. "Nevertheless death reigned from Adam to Moses, even over them that had not sinned after the similitude of Adam's transgression, who is the figure of him that was to come" (Rom. 5:14). The apostle Paul indicates in this text that, before God instituted through Moses a structured system of animal sacrifice for the forgiveness of the sins of the people, sin reigned over mankind without sacrifice. Then everyone was bow to the empire of sin. In the explanation of the plan of redemption that is to bring us into eternity, God used Moses to bring His people out of the worldly system of Egypt that they might enter the Promised Land of Canaan. Moses took them through subsequent educational stages that they might attain the spiritual maturity necessary to accomplish God's purpose for them.

Moses was brought up in the house of Pharaoh. Yet, he crossed the desert to escape the wrath of the Egyptians after he defended a Hebrew slave by taking the life of an Egyptian. In the wilderness, he witnessed the burning bush and was called of God to return to Egypt as an instrument of God to deliver His people from bondage under Pharaoh. God then promised to be with His mouth. Moses learned that he could speak to God regularly and directly. He spent forty days and forty nights on Mount Sinai in the presence of the Lord to obtain the tables of the law. Scripture reports that, on his return from the mount, the glory of God radiated from his face (Exod. 34:30). On the spiritual plane, the glory of God reflects not only on the physical appearance of a person, but it also influences the person's attitude. If the Holy Spirit takes possession of the life of a believer, He does not do so without producing an inner transformation (see Exod. 32 and 33).

Gradual Education Through Consecration

We must understand that our heavenly Father uses the same technique to educate us as we use to educate our children. At home and at school, we are obliged to take into account the age of our children in relation to the education we provide them, otherwise we are wasting our time. In the lower classes of elementary school, lessons are often associated with images to make them more concrete and to facilitate understanding. If we present a fifth-grade lesson to a child in first grade, the child will not be able to understand it because there are intermediate steps between these two levels. The opposite situation would create another difficulty. If the child is too advanced for the lesson presented to him, he will be bored. Thus, the ideal situation is for the child to progress at the rate of the instruction given by the father, mother, or teacher. In all systems of education, we notice that some students move faster than others. We may wonder what facilitates the rapid progression of some, while others take longer to advance. We know that the amount of time the student puts into study and how willing he or she is to follow the guidance of the instructor can make a big difference. You and I are God's students. The aim of this exercise is to encourage us to embark on the path of reflection.

God made two commitments to His children in two covenants. If we ask ourselves, why did God make a first covenant with His children in the Old Testament, and then a second covenant in the New Testament? Are we to believe that God made a mistake and then corrected it? We know that our God is infallible. Knowing this leads us to think that, in His greatness and immeasurable love, God had always wanted to give the second covenant. Yet, when He gave the first covenant, humankind in his spiritual journey was not yet ready to receive the second. Moreover, since certain conditions essential to the application of the new covenant were not yet in place, He used the first covenant as a preparatory step (Exod. 19:3–8; Heb. 8:6–13). In the first covenant, He gave the Ten Commandments and promised to make His people a kingdom of priests. In the second covenant, He promises to write His law in the hearts and minds of His children. We will verify the fulfillment of these promises, demonstrating whether it is true or not that divine revelation is a gradual process.

The promise of the first covenant could not be fulfilled during the times of the Old Testament. To understand the substance of God's promise, we must know who the priests were and what their function was. God chose the lineage of Aaron to serve as priests. The Greek word for "priest" is *hiereus*, which comes from the Greek word *hieros*, which means "holy." This would indicate that one who served as a priest should lead a life of sanctification. He was a mediator between God and the people, a figure of Jesus Christ. He had to make sacrifices for the sins of the people.

Let us consider the consecration ritual of the priests to better understand what God meant by His vow to make His people a kingdom of priests. According to Leviticus 8, it is, above all, a ritual of sanctification and consecration. According to the LORD's instructions, Moses began to wash Aaron and his sons and clothe them in their priestly robes. These garments were made under divine direction, and the book of Exodus reports, that the tailors were animated by the Holy Spirit who guided them to carry out the LORD's instructions. That the priests wore clothes provided by God has a special significance. In Revelation 3:4, 18, the LORD offered His children white garments, which symbolize His righteousness. We presume that the garments contributed to the process of the sanctification of the priests and that they represented the glory of God.

There was a place on the ephod of the high priest where the names of the twelve tribes of Israel were inscribed (Exod. 28:12). This signified that whenever the high priest entered the Most Holy Place, he carried the children of Israel with him. The responsibility of carrying God's people was transferred to Jesus Christ at the moment He began His ministry as high priest in the heavenly sanctuary. (See the prophecy of the 2300 days in Daniel 8 and the epistle to the Hebrews.) Jesus carries us on His bosom in the heavenly sanctuary. God "hath raised us up together, and made us sit together in heavenly places, in Christ Jesus" (Eph. 2:6). Another very significant thing is that the priest carried a sacred diadem on his forehead. On this diadem was inscribed: "Holiness to the LORD" (Exod. 39:30). It should be noted that the ceremony of consecration of Aaron and his sons was done in the tent, or tabernacle, of the congregation, built under the Lord's direction. Moses was to slaughter a bull whose blood was used to purify the Tent. Then he killed a ram for the forgiveness of the sins of Aaron and his sons. A second ram was killed for the consecration and inauguration of the priesthood and the sanctuary. Moses applied the blood of this second ram to the lobe of Aaron's right ear, to the thumb of his right hand, and to the big toe of his right foot. Moses did the same for the sons of Aaron. This divine ritual of ordination was to consecrate the priest to total obedience—the ear to hear, the hand to work, the feet to walk—to the LORD. All consecrated persons under the new covenant should seriously consider the implications of this ritual of consecration under the first covenant, for all new covenant believers are to be consecrated to God through the blood of Jesus Christ (Rom. 12:1; 1 Cor. 7:23; Rom. 6:22).

To build the earthly sanctuary, God allowed Moses to visualize the model of the sanctuary in heaven (Exod. 25:8, 9). It is important to understand that this sanctuary was necessary to present the offerings of sacrifice for sins through the sacred priesthood. More than this, the earthly sanctuary was a model for the heavenly sanctuary where Jesus Christ would minister as High Priest on behalf of believers. Without the model of the earthly sanctuary, the reality of the heavenly sanctuary would be very unclear in our minds, unless God were to imprint it in our hearts in a special way by the Holy Spirit. Through the earthly sanctuary, the Lord helps us understand what is happening in the heavenly sanctuary. The concrete explains the abstract. The heavenly sanctuary represents a more advanced stage in divine revelation as compared to the earthly sanctuary.

The Scriptures report another important truth taught by the sanctuary. When Jesus died, the veil that separated the Holy Place and the Most Holy Place was torn from top to bottom. This was a symbolic message that communicated that access to the Most Holy Place above was provided through the blood of Jesus Christ for all who desire such access and who fulfill the conditions to enter therein. This revelation brings us to a more advanced stage in Christian understanding.

Since the Exodus, God has promised to make His people "a kingdom of priests" (Exod. 19:6), that is to say, a government ruled by a king whose citizens would be sanctified and consecrated. The following statements of the apostles Peter and John show us the fulfillment of the Lord's promise to make His children a kingdom of priests (1 Peter 2:4, 5). "As you come to him, a living stone rejected by men but in the sight of God chosen and precious, you yourselves like living stones are being built up as a spiritual house, to be a holy priesthood, to offer spiritual sacrifices acceptable to God through Jesus Christ" (1 Peter 2:4, 5, ESV). "For thou wast slain, and hast redeemed us to God by thy blood out of every kindred, and tongue, and people, and nation; and hast made us unto our God kings and priests: and we shall reign on the earth" (Rev. 5:9, 10). Under the new covenant, these true priests by consecration and the blood of Jesus Christ are able to present themselves freely in the most holy place of heaven in God's presence. It is not difficult to understand that Jesus made us a kingdom of priests. We only have to realize that we are priests. A priest cannot live like other people. A priest is to lead a life of sanctification, consecrated to the service of God, and able to approach Him daily.

> *Our spiritual capacity is unlimited when the life of Jesus Christ is grafted to our life through the Holy Spirit.*

The priests wore clothes made under divine direction and the unction of the Holy Spirit. Chapters 25–40 of Exodus and chapters 1–9 of Leviticus provide information on the construction of the tabernacle, including its consecration, the clothing of the priests, and all the services and rituals that foreshadow the first coming of Christ and His ministry in the heavenly sanctuary.

The LORD instituted the Passover after the people of Israel left Egypt. The day of their liberation was of such great importance that God proclaimed it a holiday for all the people in addition to being their New Year's Day. The deliverance of Egypt was liberation not only from slavery but also from the Egyptians' moral standards and customs. "And they shall take of the blood, and strike it on the two side posts and on the upper door post of the houses, wherein they shall eat it. And they shall eat the flesh in that night, roast with fire, and unleavened bread; and with bitter herbs they shall eat it" (Exod. 12:7, 8). The sacrifices of animals that foreshadow the death of Jesus were a visible reminder that the Savior will come to help us take a step forward in our journey toward eternity in spiritual liberation from the slavery of sin and Satan.

Jesus connected Himself with the bread of heaven in the wilderness, saying:

> "I am that bread of life. Your fathers did eat manna in the wilderness, and are dead. This is the bread which cometh down from heaven, that a man may eat thereof, and not die. I am the living bread which came down from heaven: if any man eat of this bread, he shall live for ever: and the bread that I will give is my flesh, which I will give for the life of the world." (John 3:48–51)

Jesus also invites us to drink the unfermented grape juice that represents His blood (Matt. 26:28). In order for us to reflect Jesus, our life must be imbued with the life of Jesus. We are called to live our Christian life at the highest level of our spiritual capacity, and our spiritual capacity is unlimited when the life of Jesus Christ is grafted to our life through the Holy Spirit.

"For in him dwelleth all the fulness of the Godhead bodily" (Col. 2:9). "You are partners with Christ Jesus because of God. Jesus has become our wisdom sent from God, our righteousness, our holiness, and our ransom from sin." (1 Cor. 1:30, *GOD'S WORD*). If we consider ourselves as merely human, we think of the words like "impossible," "barrier," and "wall." However, if we raise our eyes toward God, the possibilities are limitless. Everything is within our reach. We have everything and can do all things because we form one and the same plant with Jesus (see John 15; Rom. 6:5).

Gradual Education by the Law

We have already discussed some matters regarding the law, specifically the two covenants. We can understand that God's desire is that we have His law written in our hearts because this action is the last educational step of His teaching in relation to the law. Yet, why did the LORD want to put His law in our heart? We must delve deeper into the meaning of the heart according to Scripture.

In Ezekiel 36:26, 27, the Lord promised to give His children a new heart and a new spirit. "I will put my spirit within you," he said, "and cause you to walk in my statutes, and ye shall keep my judgments, and do them." Therefore, the presence of God's law in our hearts must help to change our hearts and make us more apt to serve Him. When the law was on the tables of stone, one could not have it on hand at all times, unless one had a good memory. This situation helped to create formalist believers who have masqueraded as believers who have developed a relationship of love and friendship with the Creator. Thus, the first objective of God was undoubtedly to inscribe this law in our memory because it is this same law that He will inscribe in our hearts. Let us see together what God did to prepare Ezekiel before sending him on his mission.

We can understand that God's desire is that we have His law written in our hearts because this action is the last educational step of His teaching in relation to the law.

> And when I looked, behold, a hand was stretched out to me, and behold, a scroll of a book was in it. And he spread it before me. And it had writing on the front and on the back, and there were written on it words of lamentation and mourning and woe. And he said to me, "Son of man, eat whatever you find here. Eat this scroll, and go, speak to the house of Israel." So I opened my mouth, and he gave me this scroll to eat. And he said to me, "Son of man, feed your belly with this scroll that I give you and fill your stomach with it." Then I ate it, and it was in my mouth as sweet as honey. And he said to me, "Son of man, go to the house of Israel and speak with my words to them. (Ezek. 2:9–3:4)

The Lord does not send us out without giving us the necessary preparation. Jesus not only trained His disciples, but He did a miracle to signify at which step in their training they were. In the miracle of bread and fish, He asked them to pick up the remaining food, and they gathered twelve basketsful. This food was the symbol of His word and teaching. The twelve baskets represented the twelve disciples. The first disciples had received their teaching (the food) from Jesus. They had the responsibility of making other disciples for Jesus through the training they received (the bread in the twelve baskets). Today, this responsibility rests with each of us, and the first step in fulfilling our responsibility is to eat the spiritual bread.

By analogy, we can deduce that the purpose of God is that we consume His law, as our food, absorbing and digesting it, and drawing all the spiritual nutrients from it. When we absorb food, after a few hours it becomes part of us. Likewise, when the law of God is written in our hearts, it will become part of our nature. God's purpose for His Word is to enable us to act in a natural way in relation to God's law, which expresses His character and will. The law written on the tables of stone is the same as that written in the heart and mind. The law written in the heart and mind is a more advanced stage in the divine revelation, showing that the Father feels we are mature enough to enter it. Through the work of Jesus Christ, the Father fulfilled all the preconditions needed to facilitate our access to Him. It was the sacrifice of Jesus Christ that made this miracle possible.

The Prophecy of Daniel 2 and Its Progressive Aspect

I would like, in all humility, to briefly consider a lesser point from the prophecy of Daniel 2, which relates to progression. This extraordinary prophecy is of great importance with regard to the expansion of Christianity and marks a great part of the history of humanity, from the empire of Babylon 605 BC to His soon-coming return. It is a prophecy that makes us understand today that we are in the last phase of the history of this world as we know it. We are agreed that the second advent of Jesus Christ is very close. It is time to prepare. Daniel 2:34, reports that "a stone was cut out without hands, which smote the image upon his feet that were of iron and clay, and brake them to pieces." In verse 35 we read: "the stone that smote the image became a great mountain, and filled the whole earth." In the explanation of King Nebuchadnezzar's dream in verse 44, the prophet Daniel said, "And in the days of these kings shall the God of heaven set up a kingdom, which shall never be destroyed: and the kingdom shall not be left to other people, but it shall break in pieces and consume all these kingdoms, and it shall stand for ever." Verse 45 indicates that the stone that struck the statue and broke it represents the eternal kingdom that God sets up. I have verified that the majority of English and French versions of the Bible have "became" in verse 35, in "the stone became a great mountain." This raises the question: When did the kingdom of God arrive? Verse 44 sheds light with the expression: "in the time of those kings" (NIV). What do these kings represent in the statue? The legs of iron represent the Roman Empire, which was the fourth universal kingdom. Then, this kingdom was transformed into ten divided kingdoms, symbolizing the feet of iron and clay (verses 42, 43). The Semeur Study Bible, in its commentary, explains: "It is under the Roman Empire that the kingdom of God came. From then on, it grew progressively" (Semeur Study Bible, p. 1237). If we believe that the kingdom of God, in its spiritual phase, is yet future, then we will not have the sense of urgency to prepare ourselves accordingly. We Christians are already members of this divine kingdom, which has developed spiritually in preparation for its full establishment at Christ's return. This means that right now we are to behave worthy of our status as members of the kingdom of God. All indications are that the establishment of this kingdom is progressive. It seems that the first stone of this kingdom was laid down when Jesus Christ began His ministry by calling the disciples and establishing His church.

The little Robert dictionary defines the Latin of "became" as to "pass from one state to another" and to "begin to become what one was not." The Greek word translated "became" is *ginomai*, which means "to go from one state to another." To change state a certain amount of time is required. A certain amount of overlap is expected before God's spiritual kingdom, once initiated, supplants the preceding human kingdoms. We draw this conclusion from some of Jesus' statements. In Matthew 13, we find seven points about the kingdom of heaven in Jesus' parable about the mustard seed. Jesus said: "The Kingdom of Heaven is like a mustard seed planted in a field. It is the smallest of all seeds, but it becomes the largest of garden plants; it grows into a tree, and birds come and make nests in its branches" (Matt. 13:31, 32, NLT). Just as the stone, in Nebuchadnezzar's dream, needed time to become a great mountain that will fill the whole earth, so does the mustard seed also need time to grow into a big tree.

In the book, *Understanding the Difficult Words of Jesus*, David Bivin and Roy Blizzard, Jr., commented on the nearness of "the kingdom of God," using the Hebrew language. First, consider Jesus' statement, "Into whatsoever city ye enter, ... heal the sick that are therein, and say unto them, The kingdom of God is come nigh unto you.... be ye sure of this, that the kingdom of God is come nigh unto you" (Luke 10:8, 9, 11). In these two verses, Jesus repeats the term twice, "the kingdom of God is come nigh." According to Bivin and Blizzard, the term in Greek, *eggizō*, means "about to appear, almost here," while the Hebrew equivalent, *qarav* (see Hebrew of Matt. 3:2; 4:17; 10:7), means that the kingdom *has arrived*. Thus, when Jesus made this statement, the kingdom of God was already present in the world—it had arrived. Applying this understanding regarding Jesus' statements about the kingdom leads us to conclude that the return of Jesus Christ is very close in that, according to the prophecy of Daniel 2, it has been about two thousand years since the stone struck the statue. That is a very long time. From the time Jesus exercised His earthly ministry and established the Christian church, of which the first twelve disciples were the pioneers, the stone has already struck the statue. As Jesus' disciples preach the gospel and make new disciples, the stone that symbolizes the kingdom of God continues to grow until it fills the whole earth, at the time set by God, and Jesus Christ gloriously returns.

Baptism and Its Progressive Implications

To baptize in the name of Jesus Christ is to be baptized into His death (Rom. 6:3) because the baptism of Jesus Christ was itself an act that foreshadowed His death and resurrection. Through baptism, Jesus symbolized the death of the mortal body, inherited by birth, and its clothing with immortality in a new life. Yet, we note that this symbol of burial and resurrection, represented by baptism, became a reality in Jesus' life as He died and came back to life. Judging from His origin, status, and mission in fulfillment of the plan of God, we can truthfully say that Jesus had an exemplary spiritual life. That is why His baptism was the living testimony of the divine promises, insofar as the presence of the Spirit of God, by which He was conceived, was manifest in His life. His death and resurrection represent the fulfillment of the commitment made at the time of His baptism. It will be the same for us, though transformation does not take place automatically in us immediately following baptism. However, by faith and obedience to God's will, we must experience the death of our "old man," which corresponds to our burial in the water of baptism. Our arising from the water, which is equivalent to the new birth or the resurrection, follows, in the Christian journey, after the death of the "old man" and the commencement of gradual spiritual development.

> *God's system of divine education is based on a gradual educational system, progressing from simple to complex, employing images to teach more abstract concepts.*

God's system of divine education is based on a gradual educational system, progressing from simple to complex, employing images to teach more abstract concepts. One such example is the anointing oil, which symbolized the Holy Spirit. Another is the sacrifices of lambs and of the Passover lamb, which foreshadowed the death of Jesus. The priestly service foreshadowed the ministry that Jesus now exercises in the heavenly sanctuary (see Dan. 9). In Romans 7, Paul spoke of his spiritual impotence because of sin, which exercised its power in him. Paul said that, under the power of sin, he was obliged to do what he did not wish to do. He questioned aloud, "Who will deliver me from this body of death?" (Rom. 7:24, RSV). "This body of death" is a synonym for the "old man." Yet, later in his Christian journey, Paul described the progress he had made. He declared, "I am crucified with Christ: nevertheless I live; yet not I, but Christ liveth in me" (Gal. 2:20). In the epistle to the Philippians, Paul encouraged believers, "Brothers, join in imitating me, and keep your eyes on those who walk according to the example you have in us" (Phil. 3:17, ESV). Another statement of Paul's confirms the notion of spiritual progress: "Be ye followers of me, even as I also am of Christ" (1 Cor. 11:1). We can categorize some of Paul's statements as describing his carnal nature before it died and before Paul's new birth. When we understand the gradual nature of God's system of education, it will be easier for us to categorize each statement. In the first chapters of the epistle to the Romans, Paul described his struggle with the carnal man. Later in the same epistle, he spoke of himself as a new man who has undergone the new birth. He also explained his journey and the reasons for his spiritual transformation (Rom. 6:3–6; see also Gal. 2:20; 2 Cor. 12:7–10; 6:4–8; Acts 14:22; and 2 Cor. 4:8–12).

Extra-Biblical Revelations

A. Mathematics of Vertigo

José Frendelvel, in his book, "L'Or des Étoiles" reports a vast and particularly elaborate mathematical architecture highlights a troubling "signature" within the solar system. This celestial cathedral has many facets: geometry, reversed phenomena, sets of figures, among other things. Starting from a surprising arithmetic game around the number 4, which turns out to be the digital cornerstone of the solar system, this article also explains how the earth and its moon, Venus, and Mercury are incredibly linked mathematically to simple geometric figures such as the circle, the square, the triangle and the pentagon, as well as Plato's volumes.

B. The Mimicry of Sun and Moon

Since the dawn of time, the sun and the moon have been the two great luminaries of our planet, rhythmizing flora and fauna as well as the majority of human activities under millennia of cycles of days, weeks, months, and years. The approximation of their dimensions in perspective has occasionally produced spectacular solar eclipses when the moon comes in line with the sun. These two celestial bodies appear to us as a disc of 0.25 degrees (1/4) of radius. In reality, these two bodies have very different dimensions since the sun is 400 times larger than the moon in diameter. Nonetheless, since our moon is 400 times closer, the two appear to us as being of identical magnitudes. At the astronomical level, the probability of such a coincidence is very small. Yet, these two companions of day and night have beat the odds by playing with the number 4. Thanks to the observation of the spots that appear on the sun, it has been possible to measure the rotation of its visible surface known as the photosphere, which has proved to be much faster at the equator than at the poles. The exact estimation of the rotation in the polar zones is difficult, whereas the equatorial zone rotates in 25 (25.38) days. The number 25, which is the quantity of the inverse of the number 4 (since $1/4 = 0.25$), is thus a solar reference point. This period marks a sidereal rotation with respect to distant stars that can be referenced, on our human scale, as a fixed landmark. Conversely, any point on the solar equator takes 27.3 days to face the earth a second time, because our planet is also moving as it orbits the sun. This period of time is called a synodic rotation of the sun, and, quite curiously, it is equal to the period of the revolution of the moon around the earth. Yet, even more astonishing, during recent years, astrophysicists have discovered that just below the photosphere, the internal solar mass turns in one block in just over 27 days. This double synchronism of the moon and the sun is so anachronistic that the investigating scientific authorities have remained very discreet about this fact, avoiding communicating to the public a more precise value of this rotation of the sun's internal structure.

C. The Captivating Moon

Our indefatigable celestial companion does not merely mimic the size of the sun and synchronize itself with it, but it also accomplishes other feats, many of which are related to its period of sidereal revolution of 27.32166 days. To explore these feats, let us start with a simple, fun experiment.

Chapter 4 *The Divine Revelation* 63

Let us key into a calculator, the value of this lunar revolution in the most precise manner, namely 27.32166. Then let us simply press the inverse/reverse button, and the calculator will display the result as 0.036600. The first three significant digits 366 give us directly the number of rotations of the Earth in a normal, non-leap-year. In a normal calendar year, the earth makes 366 rotations. However, because it is revolving around the sun, it realizes only 365 alternations of day and night.

Calculating the inverse of a number—in this case 27.32166—amounts to the following division: $1 \div 27.32166 = 0.036600$. If we compare the period of a solar day with that of a lunar revolution, we get exactly the same equation: 1 day ÷ 27.32166 days = 0.036600. Now if one does not compare the terrestrial solar day, but, rather, the period of the sidereal rotation of the earth to that of the revolution of the moon, the equation is slightly different since the period of rotation of the earth is a little less than the 24 hours of a day. The terrestrial rotation takes place in 23 hours 56 minutes and 4 seconds, this corresponds to 0.99727 days. The equation is then: 0.99727 days ÷ 27.32166 days = 0.03650. This time the first three significant digits give us the number of days in a normal year of our calendar. The results are at once promising.

We are aware that digesting this second article may require laborious effort, but that is why we have shortened it. These two articles demonstrate not only that we are not alone on the earth but that we are part of a gigantic complex governed by specific mathematical laws. This conclusion lends itself the conclusion that the universe was planned, was constructed, and is managed by an expert Architect. This little excursion in thought has demonstrated certain realities of the universe in which we travel.

Chapter 5
A Contagious Sin

One of the key concepts in Scripture is that of sin. In this chapter, we will explore the origins of sin, its nature, its hold on humanity, and God's solution to it.

The Definition of Sin

The Bible dictionary of Vigouroux points out that the beginning of all sin is pride. The apostle James declared: "God opposes the proud but gives grace to the humble" (James 4:6, ESV). The dictionary adds: "This pride itself ... has its origin in the nature of the created being, even though not yet fallen. ... The more a created being has received gifts from the goodness of the Creator, the more reasons he has to revel in what he is and has, if his will comes to deviate from perfect rectitude" (Fulcran Vigouroux, "Péché," *Dictionnaire de la Bible*, vol. 5, part 1, col. 8). This statement is related to Ezekiel 28:14–17, which describes the beauty of Lucifer, who was, at one time, an angel of light. However, his beauty and rank went to his head and made him proud. This was the beginning of the escalation of sin. Vigouroux went on to say that "sin is therefore not in the external act, as seen by men. It is in the soul, as it appears in the eyes of

God" (*Dictionnaire de la Bible*, vol. 5, part 1, col. 8). Sin, as behavior, is a reaction that comes from the inside to the outside. The motivation for sin comes from within. To control the effect of sin, the source must be dealt with, and that is the flesh, where sin dwells, and the heart, from which evil actions are nourished before they are executed externally by our members (i.e., our hands, mouths, etc.).

In Hebrew, the noun *asham* means "trespass" or "offense." The verb *asham* means "to do wrong, offend, trespass, commit an offense, do injury, fail, be declared a criminal." The word "sin" is taken from the Greek noun *hamartia*, which comes from the Greek verb *hamartano*, which means "to miss the goal, to follow a false path, to commit a sin, to disobey the will of God" (see Luke 15:18, 21; 1 John 5:18).

Our understanding of what sin is gives rise to various interpretations regarding its gravity, its consequences, and what we believe to be God's view of it. Some people say there are several types of sins, based on the severity of the sin and the sinner's attitude. The Bible speaks of voluntary sins, involuntary sins, sins of negligence (Luke 12:48), sins of omission (Luke 11:42), and sins of ignorance. Other people think that all sins are equal because sin is always sin. I have often told friends that it is certainly better to steal someone's wallet than it is to kill him. I understand that both acts are sin. However, the difference in the gravity of these acts and in their consequences is immense. One particular viewpoint says: "God does not regard all sins as of equal magnitude; there are degrees of guilt in His estimation, as well as in that of man; but however trifling this or that wrong act may seem in the eyes of men, no sin is small in the sight of God. Man's judgment is partial, imperfect; but God estimates all things as they really are" (*Steps to Christ*, p. 29). This statement means that certain habits that we may underestimate in their magnitude can still prevent us from entering the heavenly homeland. In the Old Testament there is another factor, it seems, that is weighed in the balance of God. The motive which urged us to perform a reprehensible action. Were we aware of our behavior? Was the action a deliberate choice?

In chapter 15 of the Book of Numbers, the Lord directed Moses concerning how the priests should offer offerings for the forgiveness of the involuntary sins of the people. Verse 30 calls blasphemy against the Lord a voluntary sin. He commanded that the people who commit such sins be cut off. The author of the Epistle to the Hebrews reiterated this same idea: "For if we go on sinning deliberately after receiving the knowledge of the truth, there no longer remains a sacrifice for sins" (Heb. 10:26, ESV). The results of blasphemy are roughly the same in the Old Testament and in the New Testament. These texts do not mention grace, but neither do they exclude it. We must find the right balance between the pronouncements of God and the discernment of the Holy Spirit.

Moreover, certain sins are classified as abominations in both testaments. According to a dictionary of the New Testament by Eugene R. Pigeon, an abomination is a repulsive thing and an object of disgust and horror in the eyes of God because it occupies the place of God in the life of man. In other words, sin has not changed its name, and it is always opposed to the holiness of God. Paul considers certain sins to be faults and offenses (Gal. 6:1), which should be dealt with gently. I am not attempting to fully develop this complex subject, yet I hope that you will find encouragement in what we have considered for your spiritual journey. Sin, by its very definition, leaves a person with a desire for more, which is all the more reason for us to pursue this subject further.

The Contagious Sin of Adam and Eve

Some Christian denominations adopt the concept of "original sin" to explain humankind's corruption as inherited by nature from Adam. We discover in Scripture, how the evil of sin, which began at the tree of the knowledge of good and evil, was transmitted to the human race. In Genesis 4, the Lord Himself spoke to Cain, comparing sin to someone standing at the door, waiting for a favorable opportunity to act upon a person. The apostle Paul made ample use of the concept of sin in the Epistle to the Romans, which we, as Christians, can explore further. Let us consider some of Paul's statements about sin. Verse 12 of Romans 5 tells us, "Wherefore, as by one man sin entered into the world, and death by sin; and so death passed upon all men, for that all have sinned." Verse 23 of Romans 7 says: "But I see in my members another law waging war against the law of my mind and making me captive to the law of sin that dwells in my members" (ESV). Going further, verse 8 says: "But sin, seizing an opportunity through the commandment, produced in me all kinds of covetousness" (ESV), and verses 16 and 17 say: "Now if I do what I do not want, I agree with the law, that it is good. So now it is no longer I who do it, but sin that dwells within me" (Rom. 7:16, 17, ESV). Paul had already demonstrated that all people—Jews and Greeks alike—are under the dominion of sin (Rom. 3:9). All have sinned and are deprived of the glory of God (Rom. 3:23). "Nevertheless death reigned from Adam to Moses, even over them that had not sinned after the similitude of Adam's transgression, who is the figure of him that was to come" (Rom. 5:14). This is the spiritual death that prevailed upon humanity.

One might add that, before eating the tree of the knowledge of good and evil, evil was not yet in human nature. Yet, when Adam and Eve consumed the fruit of the tree of the knowledge of good and evil, that which Paul described took place—evil was introduced into human nature. Because we are all children of Adam by nature, that is, before the death of the "old man" and the new birth, we all inherit Adam's sinful nature. In John 3:6, Jesus told us that what is born of the flesh is flesh. The Creator God becomes our true Father the moment we undergo the death of the "old man" and escape the empire of sin to walk according to the Spirit. Nonetheless, we are still imperfect. This fact does not mean that we do not belong to God.

It is important to stress that it is impossible to understand correctly the letter to the Romans without accepting that consuming the fruit of the tree of the knowledge of good and evil introduced into human nature the binding force of sin and evil. On the other hand, if we do not grasp the reality and true meaning of the death of the "old man" that takes us from the grasp of sin to a new life in Jesus Christ, as discussed in Romans 7, it will be difficult for us to grasp the essence of Romans.

> *The death of the "old man" takes us from the grasp of sin to a new life in Jesus Christ.*

Before sin, humanity knew only good. Adam and Eve lived in a paradisiacal atmosphere, in the garden of Eden. Face to face they could see their Creator, who had formed them with His own hands. I can imagine them talking together, understanding one another, and loving one another without reserve. What more wonderful thing could there be but to find oneself in the immediate presence of God without a barrier or intermediary? When humans lived in an earthly paradise, they were only filled with good, and they were only living for good. God's presence releases a flow of inexpressible happiness. It is an attractive force that leads us towards good and engages us in the path of spiritual progress. The three persons of the Godhead are intimately connected. Certain experiences with the Holy Spirit, such as the baptism of the Holy Spirit, can give us a taste of the happiness of the presence of God.

Jealous of our happiness, Satan suddenly arose, employing the serpent as an intermediary to catch Eve's attention. Eve's decision to obey the voice of the serpent has irreversibly changed the nature of humankind and our environment. Since the word of God is certain and true, it is also action. When God speaks, the thing that He has spoken comes into existence by His command. God intended that His word be fulfilled in the life of humankind.

God said, "… The day that thou eatest thereof thou shalt surely die" (Gen. 2:17). On that fatal day when they ate the forbidden fruit, sin found its abode in the life of humankind, who were created in the image of God according to His likeness. Since then it has imposed itself as a binding force, bringing the human race more and more into corruption. In each person, sin grows rapidly and takes control. The sanctity of God's nature is hostile to sin. Therefore, the close relationship that existed between God and man has collapsed. The Creator expressed His disappointment in these words: "My spirit shall not always strive with man, for that he also is flesh: yet his days shall be an hundred and twenty years" (Gen. 6:3). A little further in the same chapter we read: "The earth also was corrupt before God, and the earth was filled with violence. And God looked upon the earth, and, behold, it was corrupt; for all flesh had corrupted his way upon the earth" (Gen. 6:11, 12). The observation is obvious—humankind has become the repository of both good and evil, and the latter has gained the upper hand. Satan seeks by all means to draw us more and more towards evil, to plunge us into sin and, at the same time, to move us away from our Creator.

Sin, a Binding Force in the Natural Man

The Lord intervened upon seeing Cain's jealousy and anger when Cain saw God's approval of his brother's offering and not his. In that situation, God addressed Cain, personifying sin as an enemy watching and waiting for an opportunity to leap on Cain. "But if you don't do what is appropriate, sin is crouching near your doorway, turning toward you. Now as for you, will you take dominion over it?" (Gen. 4:7, ISV). God felt that man still had within himself the necessary resources to dominate evil because good also dwelt in him. According to the context, we cannot equate the sin waiting at the door to act with Cain's bad behavior. It resembles rather the binding force that the apostle Paul called sin in the letter to the Romans. Anger and covetousness are among the inappropriate motivations that can lead the Christian to act according to the desires of the flesh and even obey satanic suggestions. Obviously, sin has desires; it can stand at the door of the heart. It is a dormant impulsive power whose activities vary from one person to the next. God described it as an active force that remains latent in man, waiting for just the right situation to activate itself.

Paul identified the spiritual situation of every person as being a "natural man" from birth. "We have before proved both Jews and Gentiles, that they are all under sin" (Rom. 3:9). Jesus reminded us in John 3:6a that what is born of the flesh is flesh. All the children of Adam are carnal, and sin reigns over them. The Greek word translated "reign" literally means "to be a king, to act like a king." We can deduce that the sin in Romans 5 is the evil that is in our nature, as a king—"so that, as sin *reigned* in death, grace also might reign through righteousness leading to eternal life through Jesus Christ our Lord" (Rom. 5:21, ESV). Paul referred to the situation of the carnal man, in Romans chapter 3, verse 9, declaring that all humans are under the control of sin. The power of sin has no limit as long as man remains carnal. To escape from the control of sin, one must become a spiritual son of God by appropriating all the blessings of which we are the object in Jesus Christ: redemption, justification, resurrection, and the new birth. Romans 7 deals with the solution to the domination of sin.

> For we know that the law is spiritual: but I am carnal, sold under sin. For that which I do I allow not: for what I would, that do I not; but what I hate, that do I. If then I do that which I would not, I consent unto the law that it is good. Now then it is no more I that do it, but sin that dwelleth in me. For I know that in me (that is, in my flesh,) dwelleth no good thing: for to will is present with me; but how to perform that which is good I find not. For the good that I would I do not: but the evil which I would not, that I do. Now if I do that I would not, it is no more I that do it, but sin that dwelleth in me. I find then a law, that, when I would do good, evil is present with me. For I delight in the law of God after the inward man: But I see another law in my members, warring against the law of my mind, and bringing me into captivity to the law of sin which is in my members. O wretched man that I am! who shall deliver me from the body of this death? I thank God through Jesus Christ our Lord. So then with the mind I myself serve the law of God; but with the flesh the law of sin. (Rom. 7:14–25)

In these verses, it is important to understand that Paul speaks of the condition of the unregenerated man before the death of the "old man." I took care not to use the word "conversion" because this is a progressive process. We can easily understand that Paul described in these verses his condition following his entry into Christianity and his baptism. He was in the midst of the mechanism of transformation that we call conversion. He expressed all the upheaval of conscience that he suffered. The sin that dwelt in him took control, that is, the evil inherited from Adam that represents the denigration of our nature because of disobedience. Because the natural—or carnal—man is directed above all by his carnal will, his mind is incapable of directing him according to the divine will. Paul expressed the intensity of the struggle in fighting against the sin that still remained in him.

If Romans 7 is used outside its context, one may come to conclusions besides those found in the passage. In the first three verses of chapter 8, the apostle posits a transition: "For the law of the Spirit of life in Christ Jesus hath made me free from the law of sin and death. For what the law could not do, in that it was weak through the flesh, God sending his own Son in the likeness of sinful flesh, and for sin, condemned sin in the flesh" (Rom. 8:2, 3). By sending His Son to die in this sinful flesh, God condemned sin in the flesh for all believers. Therefore, because of sin, the fleshly—or "carnal"—man in every believer is also condemned to die, in order that the source of sin might be controlled and even eliminated.

The Depravity of the Human Race

The first chapters of the epistle to the Romans describe the situation of the carnal man. They tell how sin spares no one. All people—whether Jews, Greeks, or pagans—are under sin's control. "Nevertheless death reigned from Adam to Moses, even over them that had not sinned after the similitude of Adam's transgression, who is the figure of him that was to come" (Rom. 5:14). It is evident that Paul means that even those who have not sinned in directly disobeying a divine prescription are under the influence of sin. By sin, Paul means the evil that we inherit from Adam—the inclination that drives us to do evil. Paul presented Jesus Christ as a second Adam (see 1 Cor. 15:47). Because of our natural state of sin, all humans alike need a Savior. Our heavenly Father did His part, sending us Jesus Christ. Now it is up to each person to exercise the gift of free will to choose to collaborate with the Holy Spirit in His work of transformation to reduce the influence of sin in his or her life.

A. The flesh, the abode of sin

Let us now explore, at a deeper level, what "the flesh" is. The following are definitions of the word "flesh" from a New Testament Bible dictionary. The word "flesh," from the Greek *sarx*, means: (a) the weakest element of human nature (Matt. 26:41; Rom. 6:19, 8:3a); (b) the undeveloped state of men (Rom. 7:5; 8:8, 9); (c) the seat of sin in the inner man (2 Peter 2:18; Gal. 5:24–26); (d) the inferior and temporary element in the Christian (Gal. 3:3; 6:8); (e) the human being and his natural abilities (Eph. 2:1–5).

B. The destruction of the flesh

The purpose of Jesus' sacrifice was to destroy sin. Even before the birth of Jesus, the angel of the Lord, who had come to announce the news to Joseph, had taken care to specify the Savior's main mission in Matthew 1:21: "He will save His people from their sins" (see also John 1:29). This idea is clearly expressed in Hebrews: "But now, at the end of the ages, he has appeared once for all to remove sin by his sacrifice" (Heb. 9:26b, ISV). His death has provided us with all the spiritual weapons necessary to fight evil. In Romans 6, verse 6, the verb translated "destroyed" can also be translated "cancelled." It is the Greek word *argeō* which means "abolish, suppress, annul." The Darby version of verse 6 reads: "knowing this, that our old man has been crucified with *him*, that the body of sin might be annulled, that we should no longer serve sin." The Semeur Bible translates the statement, "the old man is crucified with Jesus so that his strength is reduced to impotence." Instead of "crucified," the Louis Second Bible uses "destroyed." Why destroy the old man? Verse 7 answers: "For he that is dead is freed from sin." We can add another element to this from chapter 8: "For the sinful nature is always hostile to God. It never did obey God's laws, and it never will. That's why those who are still under the control of their sinful nature can never please God" (Rom. 8:7, 8, NLT). The death of the carnal man is a progressive work. Therefore, the more carnal we are, the more we sin; the less carnal we are, the less we sin.

The flesh prevents us from living the life that we are called to live in Jesus. It is impossible for the Spirit to accomplish His work in us, if the flesh is not tamed. "And they that are Christ's have crucified the flesh with the affections and lusts. If we live in the Spirit, let us also walk in the Spirit. Let us not be desirous of vain glory, provoking one another, envying one another" (Gal. 5:24–26; see also Eph. 2:1–5).

The Lord, through His perfect knowledge of human nature, knows full well that it is through difficulties, suffering, and the work of the Holy Spirit in the heart that the "old man" can die. It is in moments of helplessness that people, who truly devote themselves to God instead of seeking their own solution, resort to prayer and supplication to implore divine help. It is in this state of mind of complete submission that our God intervenes to strengthen and transform us.

The Antidote to Sin, the Cross, or the Death of the "Old Man"

There are forces that combine to train and keep man in sin. The most important of these are the world and its attractions, Satan and his demons, and the carnal man in the life of every believer. The world is under the dominion of the devil up to a certain point (John 16:11). By this I mean that the world and the devil agree to keep humans bound by the chain of sin. Our heavenly Father, in order to solve the problem of sin, decided to act in order to put the carnal man to death by the daily carrying of the cross (Luke 9:23). He who is dead is free from sin. "If we be dead with Christ, we believe that we shall also live with him: knowing that Christ being raised from the dead dieth no more…" (Rom. 6:8, 9). This solution seems simple: those who have died are free from sin. The converse is also true: to escape from sin's control, one must die. Do not let this thought frighten you. It is not a physical death. Rather, it is the death of the "old man." Let me put it plainly: The truth about the death of the carnal man and the new birth is essential. If we understand it in the Bible and apply it in our lives, we will be blessed. The following texts illustrate God's will in this regard. "Know ye not, that so many of us as were baptized into Jesus Christ were baptized into his death? … Knowing this, that our old man is crucified with him, that the body of sin might be destroyed, that henceforth we should not serve sin" (Rom. 6:3, 6). "For what the law could not do, in that it was weak through the flesh, God sending his own Son in the likeness of sinful flesh, and for sin, condemned sin in the flesh" (Rom. 8:3). "For when we were in the flesh, the motions of sins, which were by the law, did work in our members to bring forth fruit unto death. But now we are delivered from the law, that being dead wherein we were held; that we should serve in newness of spirit, and not in the oldness of the letter" (Rom. 7:5, 6).

These texts use baptism to present the concept and the reality of the death of the "old man" and the new birth. That which is represented by baptism must take shape—become a reality—in the life of every Christian believer. As Jesus' carrying of the cross preceded His death and resurrection, so must it be for every one of us who follow Jesus. In the truth of the cross, we will understand how Jesus' experience can be ours in the Christian journey. The death of the "old man" precedes the new birth because the new birth is a kind of spiritual resurrection.

The Solution to Sin—the Blood of Jesus Christ

Certain statements of Jesus and Paul reveal that God does not want us to sin. Jesus tells us: "Be ye therefore perfect, even as your Father which is in heaven is perfect" (Matt. 5:48). To this end, He puts His Holy Spirit within us so that we may be bound to the same plant with Jesus, according to John 15 and Romans 6:5. Our heavenly Father has implanted the life of Jesus in us so that He can transform us into His image.

A while ago, we decided to try grafting a wild plant, called a zenmorette, onto an eggplant. The graft was successful, and we harvested very good eggplants. The eggplants were like those derived from a natural eggplant. On the other hand, a graft of a bitter orange tree and a sweet orange tree does not necessarily produce fruit identical to the oranges. However, it does produce a fruit with the same flavor as an orange, though with a slightly different appearance. We recognize that human grafting is not always effective like the grafting of God who is the author of life.

Our Father intends to make our grafting into Jesus perfect. He gives us the firstfruits of the Holy Spirit, who works to gradually transform us for the final redemption at the moment of Jesus' second coming. It is essential that we have the firstfruits of the Spirit in us, for His presence in us is the sign that we are ready to move on to the next stage (Eph. 1:13, 14). The Holy Spirit keeps us and leads us to good for the glory of God. In spite of everything, if we happen to sin, we have a high priest who has been tempted as we have been and can therefore sympathize with our weaknesses. He can, with the help of His own blood, forgive us and cleanse us from all unrighteousness.

Jesus Christ is our High Priest. However, if we sin, His blood is effective in cleansing us from all our defilement. He has experienced our nature. He knows our weaknesses and our needs. His mercy is at our service. "Wherefore in all things it behoved him to be made like unto his brethren, that he might be a merciful and faithful high priest in things pertaining to God, to make reconciliation for the sins of the people. For in that he himself hath suffered being tempted, he is able to succour them that are tempted" (Heb. 2:17, 18).

Moreover, He has brought us into His bosom so that we are constantly present in Him. It is enough to address our prayers to God in the name of Christ our Redeemer, and He will intercede on our behalf with the Father by means of His blood. "Having therefore, brethren, boldness to enter into the holiest by the blood of Jesus, by a new and living way, which he hath consecrated for us, through the veil, that is to say, his flesh; and having an high priest over the house of God; let us draw near with a true heart in full assurance of faith, having our hearts sprinkled from an evil conscience, and our bodies washed with pure water" (Heb. 10:19–22).

Sin, a Crucial Issue for the Believer

Sin weakens us spiritually and takes us away from our Father. Knowing this, Satan tries to throw all kinds of distractions in our path to delay us in our Christian journey, or even to distance us from our goal through unhealthy pleasures or highly-coveted worldly attractions. There are many sources of such distractions. They can include fashion, the pursuit of wealth at any price, misuse of the Internet, or excessive use of certain electronic gadgets, not excluding television. Moreover, we may be trapped by conformity to habits unsuited to the Christian life, and we may be living on the margins of Christ's will for us without realizing it. Each time we sin, we move away from our Creator and open a breach for Satan to be a part of our life because sin is his business. "Whoever makes a practice of sinning is of the devil, for the devil has been sinning from the beginning. The reason the Son of God appeared was to destroy the works of the devil" (1 John 3:8, ESV). Contrarily, to draw God to us in the person of the Holy Spirit, we must choose sanctification and goodness, because good comes from Him.

"But if the Spirit of him that raised up Jesus from the dead dwell in you, he that raised up Christ from the dead shall also quicken your mortal bodies by his Spirit that dwelleth in you. ... For if ye live after the flesh, ye shall die: but if ye through the Spirit do mortify the deeds of the body, ye shall live." (Rom. 8:11, 13). In Ezekiel 36, verses 26 and 27, the Lord promised that He would give us a new spirit so we could serve Him. This is the promise of the Holy Spirit, whose ministry produces the new birth within us. In Hebrew, the word *ruach* can mean "spirit," "Holy Spirit," "wind," or "angel." To understand which is meant, we must consider the context and other additional information. In Greek, the word *pneuma* means "breath," "wind," "spirit," or "Holy Spirit." In other situations, the Greek language is more specific. Greek also employs specific words to identify the type of love or the type of sin being described.

Sin is an important issue in the spiritual life of every believer. It would be good to try to identify and grasp the different ways it is defined. Let us hold the spotlight on it to bring it into focus, allowing each of us to explore aspects of sin that often hide in the shadows. This clarity, once obtained, will help to develop our discernment in being able to act and react well under the complex situations of our life.

Sin is a common thing for the children of Adam. Some transgressions of the divine law seem trivial because they are so repetitive and accepted by society. Living with a sinful nature, children of Adam are inclined to adopt behaviors that oppose God and violate moral rules. The natural children of Adam have not yet had the privilege of living in a totally incorruptible body. Jesus Christ insinuated this thought in John 3:6: "That which is born of the flesh is flesh." Regarding the flesh, Paul concluded: "the mind set on the flesh is hostile toward God; for it does not subject itself to the law of God, for it is not even able to do so, and those who are in the flesh cannot please God" (Rom. 8:7, 8, NASB). Yet—glory be to God—the death of Jesus Christ and the gift of the Holy Spirit give us the means to gradually change our Adamic fleshly nature into the spiritual nature that God intended.

Unlike humans, who are drawn to sin, God finds sin odious because of its disastrous consequences: sin separates God from His children, with spiritual inertia leading them to eternal perdition if the inertia is not countered. Therefore, for great evils, great remedies must be presented. The Lord has decreed that the wages of sin is death. Yet, because of His immeasurable love, our Creator has agreed to pay the price of our crimes by the death of His Son, Jesus Christ. Nonetheless, He does require a certain contribution on our part—the death of our carnal man—as a prerequisite to being freed from sin (John 3:5–7; Rom. 6:6). Our death to the carnal man takes place, by faith, in the death of Jesus Christ. The essential conditions are that we must accept His sacrifice by faith and adhere to its reality. (John 3 and Romans 6 are explained elsewhere in this book.)

> *The death of Jesus Christ and the gift of the Holy Spirit give us the means to gradually change our Adamic fleshly nature into the spiritual nature that God intended.*

Clarification

We decided to develop this topic to shed light on a question that comes up regularly regarding our actual status as Christians. Are we justified sinners, or are we just sinners? The Bible will answer this thorny issue that is part of our daily lives. First, let us consider a familiar text. "Because all of them have sinned and are deprived of the glory of God, and are made right by grace without charge and by the redemption that exists in Yeshua The Messiah" (Rom. 3:23, 24, Aramaic Bible in Plain English). We should note that these two verses form a single sentence. If we consider the first part only, Paul's point will be incomplete and can be used out of context. Paul expresses himself within the context of the Jews not understanding whether Jesus had come to die for the Gentiles. His purpose was to show that both Jews and Gentiles are children of Adam. Therefore, they all need salvation.

There are other texts that reveal our true status as Christians. Let us take John 3:6, for example, which says: "That which is born of the flesh is flesh; and that which is born of the Spirit is spirit." Jesus told Nicodemus as He tells us: We have Adam for our father, he is carnal, and we are also carnal. To become children of God, we need to receive a new birth that comes from the Holy Spirit of God. Jesus put much emphasis on the importance of this new birth for all who want to be part of His kingdom, a kingdom that is now strictly in its spiritual phase. He did not speak of a new birth to take place upon His return. The new birth is part of our spiritual preparation as His beloved bride anticipating His return. Romans 6:3, 4 shows that we now belong to God, we are called to walk in newness of life: "Know ye not, that so many of us as were baptized into Jesus Christ were baptized into his death? Therefore we are buried with him by baptism into death: that like as Christ was raised up from the dead by the glory of the Father, even so we also should walk in newness of life." Therefore, the sinner is a person who is still in Adam. He who is in Christ Jesus is a justified sinner. The word of God obliges us to fix a high degree of sanctification and consecration to facilitate our spiritual development. If we are a good example, then we can help others in their spiritual journey. Hebrews 12:13 says, "And make straight paths for your feet, lest that which is lame be turned out of the way; but let it rather be healed." (See also John 12:36, 1 Thess. 5:5; Rom. 6:7, 14; Jer. 31:30; Ezek. 18:20.)

Chapter 6
Dying to the Law

The apostle James compared God's word and God's law to a mirror. "For if any one is a hearer of the word and not a doer, he is like a man who observes his natural face in a mirror; for he observes himself and goes away and at once forgets what he was like. But he who looks into the perfect law, the law of liberty, and perseveres, being no hearer that forgets but a doer that acts, he shall be blessed in his doing" (James 1:23–25, RSV). Though some dismiss the law as pertaining only to the Old Covenant, an understanding of the law of God is essential for all believers.

The Role of the Law of God

The law plays the same role for the heart as a mirror does for the face. It allows us to recognize that which is not right. When we see dirt on our face in a mirror, our normal reaction is to reach for the soap and water to clean our face. With the heart, this would mean reaching for the restorative justification available to the believer from the Redeemer. Those who are unaware of the divine law are not fully aware of their spiritual condition or of the reprehensibility of their behavior. The law exists to serve as

> What shall we say then? is the law sin? God forbid. Nay, I had not known sin, but by the law: for I had not known lust, except the law had said, Thou shalt not covet. But sin, taking occasion by the commandment, wrought in me all manner of concupiscence. For without the law sin was dead. For I was alive without the law once: but when the commandment came, sin revived, and I died. And the commandment, which was ordained to life, I found to be unto death. For sin, taking occasion by the commandment, deceived me, and by it slew me. Wherefore the law is holy, and the commandment holy, and just, and good. Was then that which is good made death unto me? God forbid. But sin, that it might appear sin, working death in me by that which is good; that sin by the commandment might become exceeding sinful. (Rom. 7:7–13)

The Louis Segond Bible makes this last phrase even plainer: "by the commandment it should be utterly condemned."

The word of God is the expression of His character centered on love. The Lord does not change. He is the same yesterday, today, and forever. It is His revelation that progresses according to His plan of salvation and the spiritual development of man. The purpose of the law is not to save us but to be a mirror and a guide, capable of bringing every believer to Christ. Thus, it must awaken our sense of our needing a Savior. "The Written Law was therefore a guide for us to The Messiah that we would be made right by faith" (Gal. 3:24, Aramaic Bible in Plain English). "Therefore the Law has become our tutor to lead us to Christ, so that we may be justified by faith" (Gal. 3:24, NASB). As a teacher, it shows us the way to contribute to our liberation from the slavery of sin. "For Christ is the end of the law for righteousness to everyone that believeth" (Rom. 10:4). Jesus is the end of the law. This means, according to Romans 7, that he who has met Christ, suffered the death of the "old man," and developed a strong friendship with Him will be directed by the Holy Spirit (see verses 4–6). Then the one who is directed by the Spirit cannot be accused by the law because he is no longer under sin's control (see 1 John 3:6). If we do not sin it is as though the law does not even exist. But do not let this thought confuse you. The idea that emerges from 1 John 3:6 is that Christians must be continually moving towards perfection, and the inducement to sin in their life must become increasingly rare. It is clear that we cannot sin when the Holy Spirit is guiding us. Christians are on their way to a new creation that passes through the despoiling of the carnal man, until complete transformation of our flesh at the return of Christ occurs (1 Cor. 15:51–53). Yet, this step has already begun with the death and resurrection of Jesus Christ. In regions where people live a more peaceful life, it is easy to meet those who have lived their whole lives without ever going to court or paying a fine. Whoever enters into a relationship with Jesus and becomes the same plant with Him, as the branch is connected to the vine, abides in Jesus, and Jesus also abides in that person through the Holy Spirit.

The Law and the Unfolding of the Plan of Salvation

In their book, *Understanding the Difficult Words of Jesus*, authors Bivin and Blizzard analyze what is meant by "abolish" and "accomplish" within the context and linguistic reality of Jesus' use of these terms in Matthew 5:17–20. Some biblical versions use the words "abolish," "abrogate," and "destroy" as synonyms. To elucidate the text, Bivin and Blizzard transferred the Greek into a Hebrew context (for the Gospel of Matthew employs Hebrew idioms). They reported that, in Hebrew, the idiom "I came" signifies an intention or objective. This means that Jesus came to earth with the intention of completing the law, instead of abolishing it. As a result, the revelation of the law from God's perspective reaches its height in the new covenant. God's true followers are always somewhere within the framework of the progression of the revelation of God. "Destroy" and "accomplish" are technical terms that the Rabbis used in debate. If one of them found a colleague misinterpreting a passage of Scripture, he would tell the colleague: "You *destroy* the law." Thus, Jesus was saying that He did not come to misinterpret the law or destroy it by false interpretations. In order to conform to the progression

> *Christians are on their way to a new creation that passes through the despoiling of the carnal man, until complete transformation of our flesh at the return of Christ occurs.*

of His revelation, Jesus wants to abide in our hearts and in our being. Such integration is essential before any actions result.

> For there is no respect of persons with God. For as many as have sinned without law shall also perish without law: and as many as have sinned in the law shall be judged by the law; (For not the hearers of the law are just before God, but the doers of the law shall be justified. For when the Gentiles, which have not the law, do by nature the things contained in the law, these, having not the law, are a law unto themselves: which show the work of the law written in their hearts, their conscience also bearing witness, and their thoughts the mean while accusing or else excusing one another;) (Rom. 2:11–15)

The Lord is a righteous God. His criteria of judgment are inscribed in His word. When God has inscribed His law in our hearts, we are no longer under the law. The law being imprinted in our nature, we naturally do what is right. Paul was right in saying that what matters is not a mere knowledge of the law but applying it in our lives. Doing Christ's good works is necessary for all Christians who walk towards eternal life (Rom. 8:4; Eph. 2:10).

When Are We Under the Law, According to Paul?

"For sin shall not have dominion over you: for ye are not under the law, but under grace." (Rom. 6:14). Some spiritual themes are repeated because there is a close connection between baptism, the death of the "old man," death to sin, and the realization of the new birth. Our commitment to God in the baptismal waters in the name of the Father, the Son and the Holy Spirit is a commitment to follow Jesus until the "old man" dies and the new birth takes place. Romans 7, verses 1 to 6, and Romans 6, verses 3 to 7, explain very clearly that it is the death of the carnal man that removes the believer from the hold of the law. Chapter 7 uses an analogy drawn from the conjugal relationship. This subject is of great importance and deserves to be studied carefully that we may understand it well, for chapter 7 explains a somewhat complex truth, using a familiar analogy. Whenever it was that it was enacted, the law of God is part of a process of gradual learning, with a view to progressive spiritual development. In Ezekiel, chapter 2, the angel allowed Ezekiel to read the contents of the scroll before eating it. This act symbolizes knowing and memorizing the law before integrating it in the life completely. I do not believe that God intends to miraculously imprint His law in the heart of every new believer without the believer having the opportunity to know its contents. We refer here to the ancient covenant prefaced in Exodus 19:5–8 and explained in Exodus 34:27, 28 and Deuteronomy 4:13, 14. The new covenant was predicted by Jeremiah (Jer. 31:33, 34; 32:38–40) and by Ezekiel (Ezek. 16:60–62; 34:25–31). Paul explained the new covenant in Hebrews (Heb. 8:6–13; 9:15–28; 10:11–18; 12:22–24). The LORD had promised in Jeremiah 31:33: "I will put my law in their inward parts, and write it in their hearts." This implantation is a very advanced stage in the unfolding of the plan of salvation, for it requires exceptional spiritual growth from the Christian.

The purpose of the law is to reveal the presence of sin and make it obvious to all people that sin is so serious that we need a Savior. When we are conscious of our condition, we will seek the Savior. This is why, after Peter's speech, in which he called attention to the guilt of his audience, they cried out: "What shall we do?" To which Peter replied, "Repent, and be baptized, every one of you, in the name of Jesus Christ for the forgiveness of sins" (Acts 2:37, 38, NIV). Then, not wishing humans to act by compulsion but by the teaching of His Word, God arouses the human heart to take a step towards Jesus Christ so that we can be justified by faith, the means of redemption. The death and resurrection of Jesus Christ is required to make us aware of divine grace for our sins because sin does not immediately result in death as it sometimes did in Old Testament times. We always have the possibility of correcting ourselves, unless our actions are of such a grave nature that they merit, in the eyes of God, a sentence comparable to that of Amalek (Exod. 17:14). Thus, to free ourselves from the stranglehold of sin, the death of the "old man" substitutes for physical death through the symbol of baptism and the subsequent work of the Holy Spirit in the life of the genuine Christian. Before Jesus came, there was no escaping sin's grip. Now, thanks to the miracle of redemption, it is possible to destroy the carnal man in which sin resides (Rom. 6:6; Eph. 2:3; Gal. 5:24–26). According to what the apostle explained in Romans 7, as long as our carnal nature is in control of our lives, causing us to sin, the law can accuse us because we are still under the jurisdiction of our carnal nature.

Dying to Sin and Living for God in Christ

The sovereign Lord, who is the creator and provider of all things, has decided, in His righteousness, that the wages of sin should be death (Gen.

2:17; Rom. 6:23). Thus, there is a price to pay for sin and its destructiveness. To remain faithful to His principles while still being a God of love, goodness, and mercy, God sent His Son, Jesus Christ, to die for all humankind. No matter one's social standing or state of depravity, a person has the opportunity to be justified by accepting Christ as his or her personal Lord and Savior (John 3:16).

A better question than "Are we under the law?" is "What stage are we at in our Christian journey?" I say this because the second covenant is simply a more advanced stage than the first. In the second, the law is no longer on tables of stone, exposed to the eyes of all, but inscribed in each person's heart and mind. Each person has a responsibility before God. There is potentially confusing information in Romans chapter 7, verses 1–6.

Know ye not, brethren, (for I speak to them that know the law,) how that the law hath dominion over a man as long as he liveth? For the woman which hath an husband is bound by the law to her husband so long as he liveth; but if the husband be dead, she is loosed from the law of her husband. So then if, while her husband liveth, she be married to another man, she shall be called an adulteress: but if her husband be dead, she is free from that law; so that she is no adulteress, though she be married to another man. Wherefore, my brethren, ye also are become dead to the law by the body of Christ; that ye should be married to another, even to him who is raised from the dead, that we should bring forth fruit unto God. For when we were in the flesh, the motions of sins, which were by the law, did work in our members to bring forth fruit unto death. But now we are delivered from the law, that being dead wherein we were held; that we should serve in newness of spirit, and not in the oldness of the letter.

The passage reveals that we need a more spiritual relation to the law. Such a relation should guide us more effectively, thanks to our new nature acquired in Christ, expressed by a sincere love for God and our neighbor.

"For the mind that is set on the flesh is hostile to God, for it does not submit to God's law; indeed, it cannot. Those who are in the flesh cannot please God. You, however, are not in the flesh but in the Spirit, if in fact the Spirit of God dwells in you. Anyone who does not have the Spirit of Christ does not belong to him" (Rom. 8:7–9, ESV). We have mentioned that the old man must die because he is useless to God. "How shall we, that are dead to sin, live any longer therein?" (Rom. 6:2). Death to sin requires the death of the "old man," breaking sin's link in us, where sin has made its abode. Thus, if the Holy Spirit gradually destroys the carnal man, we cannot help but gradually die to sin (see Rom. 6:7, 11).

How to Be Released from the Grip of the Law, According to Paul

In verses 1 to 3 of Romans 7, Paul compares the law to a husband who holds power over his wife as long as she lives. The only escape from the control of her husband for the woman, who represents the believer, is to die. In some French and English versions, the first words in Romans 7, verse 2, are "for example." Thus, Paul used the relationship between a married man and woman as an example to explain the relationship between the law and the believer. As he said in verse 2, if believers are not dead, they remain under the authority of the law because they will continue to sin and the law will remain to accuse them. However, if the husband were to die, the woman would be free (v. 3). It is the same for you, my brothers (v. 4), when you have been put to death with regard to the law by the body of Christ so that you can belong to another, the one who is risen from the dead, that you may bear fruit for God. Verse 4 begins with a theme that expresses a comparison between a familiar situation in human life and another of spiritual significance. Paul borrowed this technique from Jesus Christ, who used parables to help His audience discover hidden truth. To understand what the apostle wanted to say to us, let us consider verse 4 in the Semeur Bible. "It is the same for you my brethren: by the death of Christ, you also are dead with respect to the law, to belong to another, He that is risen from the dead, that we may bear fruit unto God." The complexity of Romans 7 comes from the fact that the law is compared to a husband who holds authority over his wife, when the wife represents the believer. However, in verse 4, Paul makes it clear that it was the believer, who represented the woman, who must die if he wants to belong to Jesus Christ. To this end, God the Father has united us to Christ so that the death of our "old man" could be associated with Jesus' death, allowing Him to eliminate our sinful humanity. Then, when He rose in newness of life, we too are called to resurrect in spirit, or be born again, that we may lead a new life and be married to Jesus Christ.

We have already stated that the death of the husband (the law) would free his wife from the marriage covenant. However, since the husband represents the law, it is the woman, who represents the believer, that must die to free herself from the authority of her first husband. Not grasping this fact has kept many from understanding chapter 7. Like Christ, whose resurrection followed His death, so the new birth succeeds the death of the carnal man. Then, the creature, newly created by the progressive work of the Holy Spirit, is able to live according to the Spirit's directives (see the prophecy of Ezek. 36:26, 27). Therefore, when the believer's "old man," or carnal man, is dead, the believer can live according to the Spirit. When external temptations come to arouse in him the will to sin, with his "old man" dead, he can remain passive in the face of incentives, temptations, and provocations because the source of sin has been destroyed. This is explained in Romans 7, verses 4 to 6.

> *With his "old man" dead, he can remain passive in the face of incentives, temptations, and provocations because the source of sin has been destroyed.*

Let me digress briefly to introduce a subject that will be developed later. We were put to death by the body of Jesus Christ because, at our baptism, we participated in His death by faith (Rom. 6:6; 7:4). All this is possible because our heavenly Father brought us into the person of Jesus Christ, through His body, as He passed through Mary's womb. The death of the body of Jesus in which we participated will make the death of our "old man" possible through our personal experiences and the work of the Holy Spirit (see 1 Peter 4:1, 2).

The apostle concluded: "For sin shall not have dominion over you: for ye are not under the law, but under grace" (Rom. 6:14). Therefore, the death of Jesus Christ for humanity allows the death of the carnal man to be the price paid by the sinner to reduce the influence of the flesh in his life. Under the new covenant, each Christian's "old man" is marked for destruction so that the Christian is freed to walk according to the Spirit. This must be done in accordance with the divine law that should be imbued in the nature of every true believer. Our actions will prove whether or not the divine precepts are actually inscribed in our hearts. Paul earlier declared that faith does not nullify the law but confirms it (Rom. 3:31). Since it is true that Christians are justified by faith, all new believers must enter this process of education and grasp the understanding of the law that leads to Christ until they undergo the death of the "old man" to escape the constant accusations of the law.

Chapter 6 *Dying to the Law*

In 1 Corinthians 15:45, 47, Paul calls Jesus Christ the "last Adam." The Bible presents Adam as the father of the whole human race, making his sin ours, and Adam's nature is our nature, also making his sin ours (see John 3:3: Rom. 5:12). Now, through the Son of God, we are to escape the influence of the first Adam to submit to the influence of the second Adam. The difference between these two Adams is that the first Adam is earthly, and the second Adam is heavenly. The first brought sin upon the human race; the second brings life to all who believe. God permitted Jesus Christ to pass into the womb of Mary to clothe Himself with human nature that He might die in our place and save us. "And they that are Christ's have crucified the flesh with the affections and lusts [French, passions and desires]" (Gal. 5:24; see Rom. 8:3, 4).

We can deduce that, according to Romans 7, the person who is not under the law is the one whose "old man" is destroyed. Paul tells us: "Dear brothers and sisters, when I was with you I couldn't talk to you as I would to spiritual people. I had to talk as though you belonged to this world or as though you were infants in the Christian life. I had to feed you with milk, not with solid food, because you weren't ready for anything stronger. And you still aren't ready" (1 Cor. 3:1, 2, NLT), because you are too carnal. Compare Paul's statement with that of Jesus Christ. Addressing the disciples, He said: "I have yet many things to say unto you, but ye cannot bear them now. Howbeit when he, the Spirit of truth, is come, he will guide you into all truth: for he shall not speak of himself; but whatsoever he shall hear, that shall he speak: and he will shew you things to come" (John 16:12, 13). This text demonstrates that the disciples had not reached the maturity necessary to receive a more advanced revelation when Jesus was present with them. It took them time to digest the teachings of Jesus Christ and to appropriate them with the help of the Holy Spirit. They needed time to develop. According to Romans 7, it is extremely difficult for a new believer to say that, because of the new covenant, he is totally free from the law, while he has not yet suffered the death of the carnal man and been born again to be subject to the spiritual authority of the law. Through the ages, the Lord has used the technique of gradual training with the human race until the revelations concerning the plan of salvation are complete. "God presented Him as an atoning sacrifice through faith in His blood, in order to demonstrate His righteousness, because in His forbearance He had passed over the sins committed beforehand. He did this to demonstrate His righteousness at the present time, so as to be just and to justify the one who has faith in Jesus" (Rom. 3:25, 26, BSB). A spiritual five-year-old child who makes a mistake cannot be treated in the same way as a spiritual eighteen-year-old. This text might imply that, at one time, God had to be very patient with sinners because He was aware that they did not have all the tools necessary to overcome sin, since the revelations they had of His character and plan for redemption were fragmentary.

The one who is dead is free from sin, according to Romans 6, verses 6 and 7. The *New Living Translation* study Bible wonderfully explains Romans 7. Let us begin with verse 2 to illustrate. The study Bible comments that Paul used the example of marriage to explain our relationship with the law. The law cannot accuse us because we were dead with Jesus. Since that time, we have been united with Christ, and His Spirit enables us to produce good works for God. However, the law cannot disappear. In Romans 7, verse 7, Paul explains that it was only by the law that he knew sin. For he would not have known covetousness had not the law said, "Thou shalt not covet" (Rom. 7:7). Before Christ came, His blood had not yet been shed for sin, and neither had Pentecost yet taken place to give us free spiritual access to the various divine blessings. Therefore, the spiritual possibilities were more limited than they are today.

Clarification

As a side note, we should say that, to gain a better understanding of God's Word, it is important to consider the biblical passage in context, otherwise it is certain that it will be interpreted incorrectly. The apostle Paul speaks of circumcision, which was no longer necessary after the death and resurrection of Jesus. It was part of the ceremonial prescriptions which were the shadow of things to come, that is, those services that foreshadowed the sacrifice of Christ and His ministry on our behalf in the heavenly sanctuary. This is what Paul was discussing when he wrote: "You have been severed from Christ, you who are seeking to be justified by law; you have fallen from grace" (Gal. 5:4, NASB). We have already explained with supporting texts that the role of the law is to lead us to Christ. When, by the power of the Holy Spirit, we establish and maintain a relationship of abiding in Christ with the Holy Spirit whom God placed within us, we will no longer need to repeatedly return to the stone tables to inquire what the law says. On the other hand, if we apply ourselves to keeping the law formally without developing a relationship with Jesus, we will be living externally, on the fringes. However, when Christ is in us, His Word, which is our study, will be imprinted within us.

Jesus told the woman at the well, "But the hour cometh, and now is, when the true worshippers shall worship the Father in spirit and in truth: for the Father seeketh such to worship him" (John 4:23). The apostle Paul expounds on the same theme when he wrote: "… we should serve in newness of spirit, and not in the oldness of the letter" (Rom. 7:6). The bar is raised higher with the new covenant. We are invited to banish the formalist side of worship that we may have the awareness of the presence of God when we worship Him. Having the real presence of God in mind as we worship, our services will be centered on reverence, humility, and respect.

We have already pointed out, according to the writings of Paul, when it is that a believer in the Christian journey is no longer under the law. Yet, we return to this subject to be able to clarify an important truth, which has been an impediment for some experienced teachers of the Word. We would remind the reader of what Paul said about the law: "Well then, am I suggesting that the law of God is sinful? Of course not! In fact, it was the law that showed me my sin. I would never have known that coveting is wrong if the law had not said, 'You must not covet.'" (Rom. 7:7, NLT). If the law did not exist, we would not have recognized the presence of sin. The apostle Paul also praised the law: "Wherefore the law is holy, and the commandment holy, and just and good" (Rom. 7:12). Under the new covenant, our heavenly Father wants His law to be present in our hearts, that is, in our memory and guiding our conscience. This means that Christians enjoy greater blessings as time proceeds and the plan of salvation is further unfolded. From the infusion of His law in our hearts and minds, we can deduce that our Father has higher spiritual expectations of His children.

"What shall we say then? Shall we continue in sin, that grace may abound? God forbid. [Far from it!] How shall we, that are dead to sin, live any longer therein?" (Rom. 6:1, 2). "What then? shall we sin, because we are not under the law, but under grace? God forbid. [Far from it!]" (Rom. 6:15). From verse 14 we can say that Jesus took us out from under the influence of sin and, at the same time, out from under the condemnation of the law, to be able to place us under the shelter of grace. It is up to us to live as someone under grace, as described by the apostle Paul.

"For sin shall not have dominion over you: for ye are not under the law, but under grace" (Rom. 6:14). "For he that is dead is free from sin" (v. 7). It is clear that verse 7 tells us that the death of the carnal man removes us from the authority of sin. The embodiment of "sin" is used to describe the binding force in human nature. "Being then made free from sin, ye became the servants of righteousness" (v. 18). Though, according to Romans 6:3–6, we are freed from sin, according to verse 11, we must overtly consider ourselves as dead to sin, yielding our members to God that He may produce in us works of righteousness for His glory. When we do so by faith, the Holy Spirit will assist us.

To complete this subject, we will consider some texts from Galatians 5. "For all the law is fulfilled in one word, even in this; Thou shalt love thy neighbour as thyself" (Gal. 5:14). Here the apostle Paul wrote the Galatians in keeping with Jesus' statement in Matthew 19:17–19. He did not mention the first and great commandment of loving God with all our heart, soul, and mind as Jesus had in Matthew 22:37–40. "Jesus said unto him, Thou shalt love the Lord thy God with all thy heart, and with all thy soul, and with all thy mind. This is the first and great commandment. And the second is like unto it, Thou shalt love thy neighbour as thyself. On these two commandments hang [depend] all the law and the prophets" (Matt. 22:37–40). This was probably because he was speaking in a strictly human context (see v. 15). We all agree that, without love for God, man lives outside the plane of salvation.

Paul invites us to walk according to the Spirit, for, when we walk according to the Spirit, we do the will of the Spirit instead of our carnal will. "But I say, walk by the Spirit, and you will not gratify the desires of the flesh. For the desires of the flesh are against the Spirit, and the desires of the Spirit are against the flesh, for these are opposed to each other, to keep you from doing the things you want to do" (Gal. 5:16, 17, ESV). "But if you are led by the Spirit, you are not under the law" (v. 18). If we do indeed walk according to the Spirit, we will live in accordance with the law, and it will have no reason to accuse us. It will be as if it is non-existent because we are under the jurisdiction of the Holy Spirit.

Verses 19–21 list some reprehensible behaviors that are described as "the works of the flesh." Verse 22 lists behaviors that are "the fruit of the Spirit." Verse 23 tells us that the law is not against the fruit of the Spirit. Verse 24 concludes: "And those who belong to Christ Jesus have crucified the flesh with its passions and desires" (RSV).

Chapter 7
The Cross

Paul wrote: "But God forbid that I should glory, save in the cross of our Lord Jesus Christ, by whom the world is crucified unto me, and I unto the world" (Gal. 6:14). So what does the cross signify?

The Meaning of the Cross in the Life of the Believer

God is sovereign in His decisions and in the way He proceeds to solve human problems. Moreover, it is He who formed us. He knows perfectly well what we are made of. It is He who recognized that it is the cross alone, under the power of the Holy Spirit, that can destroy the carnal man and revive the spirit of man.

In Old Testament times, the cross was an object of reproach and dishonor, which symbolized the curse of the law (Deut. 21:23). No one wanted to associate with it because it was reserved for the hanging of notorious thieves and great criminals. It was used to further lower these social pariahs and rejects of society. Therefore, human beings created by Jesus Christ, as influenced by the enemy, wanted to despise and degrade Him by nailing Him to the cross. Yet, His death on the cross made the cross something beautiful and noble. It would never be seen the same.

In some countries, people who wish to identify with Jesus Christ on the cross imitate Christ's crucifixion by allowing themselves to be scourged and nailed to a cross at Easter time.

Now believers are proud to have beautiful pictures of the cross at home or a small cross on a necklace. The cross has become the path of glory, the path of spiritual regeneration, and the path of life. Paul said it so well in Philippians, that, because Jesus "humbled himself, and became obedient unto death, even the death of the cross....God also hath exalted him ..." (Phil. 2:8, 9). Thus, the ignominy of the cross precedes its glory. This was the case for Jesus Christ, and He asks us to follow Him along the same path. The cross is an obligatory part of the Christian's journey. It is comparable to a traveler entering an island country. If he gets there by boat, he must go through the quay. If he travels by plane, he must pass through the airport. These are unavoidable control points. If we arrive at our destination without all the required documents, the customs officers will send us back to our point of departure. All our documents must be in order to pass on to the next step. It is the same with the cross. Each believer who seals his or her covenant with Jesus Christ by baptism will have to pass through the stage of the cross in his or her Christian journey. The cross is not simply two crossing pieces of wood; it is a process in which the Holy Spirit uses the daily difficulties to gradually reduce the power of the carnal man in our life (see Luke 9:23).

> *The cross is not simply two crossing pieces of wood; it is a process in which the Holy Spirit uses the daily difficulties to gradually reduce the power of the carnal man in our life*

The Cross, the Foundation of Christianity

It has been reported that, in the year 312 AD, Constantine had a vision of a cross of light superimposed over the sun in heaven and that he heard the words: *en toutō nika* (Latin, *in hoc signo vinces*), which translates as "by this sign you will conquer." He adopted the cross as the emblem for his army. He was so successful with his army that he became the master and ruler of all Europe and western Asia ("Calvary," *Thompson's Study Bible*, p. 1787). Jesus Christ introduced a power in this symbolism. Chapters 40 to 42 of the book of Ezekiel report the prophet's vision of a new temple.

In the visions of God brought he me into the land of Israel, and set me upon a very high mountain, by which was as the frame of a city on the south. And he brought me thither, and, behold, there was a man, whose appearance was like the appearance of brass, with a line of flax in his hand, and a measuring reed; and he stood in the gate. And the man said unto me, Son of man, behold with thine eyes, and hear with thine ears, and set thine heart upon all that I shall shew thee; for to the intent that I might shew them unto thee art thou brought hither: declare all that thou seest to the house of Israel. (Ezek. 40:2–4)

Some Bibles carry a diagram of the base of the building produced according to the divine directions revealed to Ezekiel. It is surprising that the base of the church is the form of a cross. It should be noted that the plan for this temple is not that of Solomon's temple, nor was it that of the temple built after Israel's exile. This is surprising since we know that the cross was not a symbol for God's people until the death of Jesus Christ on a cross.

Thus, this prophetic vision points symbolically to the cross as the foundation of the church of Jesus Christ. In Christianity, the cross is unavoidable. This brings us to a statement of Jesus Christ in which three out of four of its verbs are imperative. "If any man will come after me, let him deny himself, and take up his cross daily, and follow me" (Luke 9:23). If the verbs are imperative, that means that it is more than a recommendation of Jesus Christ. It is a command. Unlike the other Gospels, Luke adds "daily" in this statement. This addition is an indication that the cross is a symbol that represents the daily difficulties in the path of the believer. A person cannot be asked to drag a real cross every day of his or her life. When Jesus made this suggestion to the twelve, they would have immediately thought of death. Because the image that was associated with the cross of Jesus was His death, and we can understand their thinking in this way. Most of the twelve disciples followed Jesus in martyrdom because of their preaching of the gospel. However, the symbol of the cross had another object, that of bringing all believers to the death of their old man to make them fit for communion with God. If the cross did not refer to the way of following Jesus, in the sense of self-renunciation and the death of the "old man," the great number of Christians who came after the great apostolic movement would have nothing to do with the cross since they did not experience persecution in their lives from the preaching of the gospel. We have seen the relationship between the death of the carnal man and baptism by immersion, the order and example of which were given by Jesus Christ, "Therefore, go and make disciples of all the nations, baptizing them in the name of the Father and the Son and the Holy Spirit" (Matt. 28:19, NLT).

Being baptized in the name of the Father and of the Son and of the Holy Spirit entitles us to justification through the blood of Jesus. It gives us the right to participate in the divine nature. It gives us the right to the presence of the Holy Spirit within us. However, it also gives God the right, in the person of the Holy Spirit, to intervene in our lives and make the necessary corrections to our lives that His blessings may take place in us.

The Role of the Cross or Difficulties

The role of the cross is to weaken the grip of the carnal man and allow the spirit of man to take over. It aims to produce a viable spiritual transformation in the life of the believer. In the unregenerated man, the "old man" is in charge. This is what the Lord meant in Genesis 6, verse 3 when He said that "man is but flesh." Verse 5 adds, "The LORD saw that the wickedness of man was great in the earth, and that every intention of the thoughts of his heart was only evil continually" (ESV). Later, in Genesis 8, verse 21, the Lord said that the thoughts of the heart of man are evil from his youth. At the beginning of this paragraph, we took care to choose the verb "to weaken" because we understand that it is at the moment of our complete transformation at the second coming that we lose our "old man" completely. However, the difficulties encountered in our Christian journey are permitted to discipline and correct the reprehensible deviations of our natural and spontaneous emotions. Paul, in his epistle to the Romans, explained why God seeks to kill the flesh. "God sending his own Son in the likeness of sinful flesh, condemned sin in the flesh. Because the carnal mind is enmity against God: for it is not subject to the law of God, neither indeed can be" (**Rom. 8:3, 7**). By bringing Jesus Christ into the womb of Mary, the Lord has introduced the whole human race into Jesus Christ. Then, by His death, He condemned sin in the flesh. It is in this sense that Paul called Jesus Christ "a second Adam coming from heaven" (1 Cor. 15:47, Louis Segond Bible). Sin is condemned in the flesh by Jesus Christ's suffering of physical death. However, for believers to be conformed to the reality of the death of Jesus, we must suffer the death of the carnal man. It is with that death that we will be born again to become conformed to the reality in which Jesus, the Messiah, was resurrected to a new life (Rom. 6:4, 5).

Chapter 7 *The Cross*

> What should we say, then? Should we go on sinning so that grace may increase? Of course not! How can we who died as far as sin is concerned go on living in it? Or don't you know that all of us who were baptized into union with the Messiah Jesus were baptized into his death? Therefore, through baptism we were buried with him into his death so that, just as the Messiah was raised from the dead by the Father's glory, we too may live an entirely new life. For if we have become united with him in a death like his, we will certainly also be united with him in a resurrection like his. We know that our old natures were crucified with him so that our sin-laden bodies might be rendered powerless and we might no longer be slaves to sin. For the person who has died has been freed from sin. Now if we have died with the Messiah, we believe that we will also live with him, for we know that the Messiah, who was raised from the dead, will never die again; death no longer has mastery over him. For when he died, he died once and for all as far as sin is concerned. But now that he is alive, he lives for God. In the same way, you too must continuously consider yourselves dead as far as sin is concerned, but living for God through the Messiah Jesus. Therefore, do not let sin rule your mortal bodies so that you obey their desires. Stop offering the parts of your body to sin as instruments of unrighteousness. Instead, offer yourselves to God as people who have been brought from death to life and the parts of your body as instruments of righteousness to God. (Rom. 6:1–13, ISV)

In the remainder of chapter 6, Paul demonstrated how the state of sin is an empire that governs our "members," that is, our "flesh." Nonetheless, in the first part of the chapter, he said that we cannot "go on living in" sin since we were baptized in the name of Jesus Christ. As God has put us in Jesus Christ, our baptism is connected to the death of Jesus Christ. So, at our baptism, our carnal body was buried in connection with the death of Jesus Christ.

It is crucial that we ask how this reality is to take place in the life of the believer. It is the Holy Spirit's task to produce this transformation in our lives in a progressive way, by passing through decisive stages, such as baptism by immersion, the baptism of the Holy Spirit, the death of the "old man," the new birth, etc. To this we would draw attention to a very important point that will provide for other insights in this book. For this transformation in our lives to be possible, in spite of the difficulties encountered along his or her pathway, the believer must remain in the will of God. This means that he or she must not, when faced with difficulty, seek to take a short cut that is contrary to the will of God. In such difficult situations, it is best to seek God through prayer.

God has vowed to destroy the "old man" who imprisons our mind and prevents us from communicating with God. Jesus told the woman at the well: "God is a Spirit: and they that worship him must worship him in spirit and in truth" (John 4:24). Therefore, God has sent the Holy Spirit to rescue our spirit, give it new birth, and free it from the guardianship of the carnal man who is doomed to destruction (John 3:6b; 2 Cor. 4:16).

> *God has decided to solve the problem of sin by the suffering of the flesh.*

The apostle Peter expounds upon the same point, speaking of the role of the cross, or suffering, in the process of the death of the "old man" and in the new birth in the life of every believer. "For Christ also hath once suffered for sins, the just for the unjust, that he might bring us to God, being put to death in the flesh, but quickened by the Spirit" (1 Peter 3:18). "Forasmuch then as Christ hath suffered for us in the flesh, arm yourselves likewise with the same mind: for he that hath suffered in the flesh hath ceased from sin; that he no longer should live the rest of his time in the flesh to the lusts of men, but to the will of God" (1 Peter 4:1, 2). The text is clear: Christ was dead with regard to the flesh, and He was resurrected with regard to the Spirit. We have been called to follow the same pattern. Peter and Paul both declare: the flesh must suffer in dying to sin. God has decided to solve the problem of sin by the suffering of the flesh. The role of the cross and of difficulties is to produce the destruction of the carnal man.

Once the power of the carnal man diminishes, the believer can live according to the Spirit. Our Father entrusts this laborious work to the Holy Spirit, according to John 3:6b. To better understand how this works, let us analyze 2 Corinthians 4:8–12:

> We are troubled on every side, yet not distressed; we are perplexed, but not in despair; persecuted, but not forsaken; cast down, but not destroyed; always bearing about in the body the dying of the Lord Jesus, that the life also of Jesus might be made manifest in our body. For we which live are alway delivered unto death for

Jesus' sake, that the life also of Jesus might be made manifest in our mortal flesh. So then death worketh in us, but life in you.

The Interlinear Greek-French New Testament translates the word "dying" in the phrase, "always bearing about in the body the dying of the Lord Jesus," as "agony." This would imply that our body is undergoing the slow death of the carnal man. Since we were baptized into the death and resurrection of Jesus Christ (Rom. 6:3–6), we must live in conformity to the life of Jesus whom the Holy Spirit implants within us. Progress in the death of the carnal man corresponds to progress in our spiritual resurrection and new birth as believers.

Carrying One's Cross to Follow Jesus

We have taken care to explain that the cross was an object of humiliation for Jesus' contemporaries. Taking up the cross meant taking the walk of death—a death that was at first sight physical. Yet, in the epistle to the Romans, the apostle Paul explained the true meaning of the cross. The cross is to lead to the death of the "old man." This means that the cross is the lot of every believer who chooses to follow Jesus Christ. According to Luke 9:23, in every age, all who want to follow Jesus are obliged to renounce themselves and take up their cross each day so they may be able to follow Him.

When my wife and I were expecting our first child, I was very excited. I made all the necessary preparations in anticipation of the baby's arrival. Then, the expected time came, and the baby was born. My joy was great until I discovered that our child suffered from an incurable disease. Until the day of my great disappointment, like every young adult, I floated on a cloud and looked at life through rose-colored glasses. At the moment of the doctor's announcement, my spirit left me deflated like an empty hot-air balloon, and my feet came crashing back down to earth. My wife and I were in a desert with no one to help us. Doctors, money, and friends could do nothing. At times, confusion swallowed me, increasing my suffering. I did not have all the spiritual resources that I have now to carry this enormous burden.

It was at that time that I began escaping to the mountain to seek the presence of God. I had to take time off from my work and go to a place where I could devote myself to prayer. By taking this path, the Eternal God sent several messages to enlighten me on what had happened and what was to come. The most explicit message came from a co-worker who was not a practicing Christian. This experience was an important part of my cross, and I had to bear it because there was no shortcut I could take. It was only after a few years when I began to understand God's loving plan for His children and began to understand why God allowed these trials in our life. At times He has shown us the danger that could have taken our lives were it not for His omnipotent protection. These personal experiences were meant to increase our confidence in Him and foster our developing relationship with Him.

None of us likes to find ourselves in difficult situations. I do not know about you, but, when I went to school, I did not like encountering difficulty. At work, all I wanted to do is have a pleasant day without incident. In church, I aspire to happiness. Nonetheless, we are often disappointed and frustrated in our endeavors. We do not expect failure, rejection, disappointment, humiliation, and insult. Albeit, we should accept whatever our cross of suffering, in calmness and reverence, as a blessing from God. Often an unexpected situation occurs, causing a conflict with our dominant nature and spoiling our day. If it is something we resist, we have to face the challenge again. This is how we gain patience and wisdom. When a mountain of difficulties presents itself before the believer who wants to remain attached to Jesus, he or she will have no other choice but to hang on, for he cannot face the challenge alone. God's promise is: "There hath no temptation taken you but such as is common to man: but God is faithful, who will not suffer you to be tempted above that ye are able; but will with the temptation also make a way to escape, that ye may be able to bear it" (1 Cor. 10:13). This means that, if a believer has traits of authoritarianism, anger, or pride, his heavenly Father, in His plan of love for him, will test his reprehensible traits to help him get rid of them. The Holy Spirit has the responsibility of keeping the trials coming until the undesirable trait in the believer has been transformed. As Jesus Christ was humbled before being glorified, so must each believer encounter difficulties to bring about the death of the carnal nature that he or she might be spiritually reborn and glorified in the end when Jesus returns.

Our heavenly Father who created us knows us better than we do ourselves. He knows how we react when we are in abundance, and He knows how we react in times of scarcity, difficulty, and disease. He knows what can bring us to Him and what can take us away from Him. It is for this reason that He gives His Spirit the responsibility of providing us with a progressive spiritual education for our gradual transformation. The education He orders is tailored to each individual's needs. The apostle Paul was a scholar. Yet, despite the excellence of his knowledge and his first experience with Jesus on the road to Damascus, the Lord had to let him go through many difficulties to purify his character and make him humble. After he became a believer in Christ, as a spiritual baby, Paul described himself as a weak man whose members were under the influence of the empire of sin. Yet, after he was truly converted and transformed, he wrote in Galatians 2:20, "I am crucified with Christ: nevertheless I live; yet not I, but Christ liveth in me," and then he was able to present his experience as an example for others (1 Cor. 11:1; Phil. 3:17; 2 Thess. 3:7–9). If the epistle to the Romans brings to mind a facet of life that is less than ideal, then God will always use the same techniques to accomplish the same results four His children: our spiritual transformation.

> So to keep me from becoming conceited because of the surpassing greatness of the revelations, a thorn was given me in the flesh, a messenger of Satan to harass me, to keep me from becoming conceited. Three times I pleaded with the Lord about this, that it should leave me. But he said to me, "My grace is sufficient for you, for my power is made perfect in weakness." Therefore I will boast all the more gladly of my weaknesses, so that the power of Christ may rest upon me. For the sake of Christ, then, I am content with weaknesses, insults, hardships, persecutions, and calamities. For when I am weak, then I am strong. (2 Cor. 12:7–10, ESV)

Like Paul, we must follow biblically ordained strategies to confront situations of trouble, affliction, and distress. We must remain attached to Jesus, who alone can give us inner peace. When our carnal man grows weaker, our spiritual nature grows stronger, as the apostle Paul pointed out. "For our light affliction, which is but for a moment, worketh for us a far more exceeding and eternal weight of glory; while we look not at the things which are seen, but at the things which are not seen: for the things which are seen are temporal; but the things which are not seen are eternal" (2 Cor. 4:17, 18). Whatever difficulty we face today, a moment spent in the glorious presence of God will make us forget all the pain that marked our Christian journey.

The parable is told of two slaves who were each commanded by their master to carry a large cross. The crosses were so heavy that they could drag them only with difficulty. Yet, the two slaves had two different attitudes about their burdens. The first resigned himself to the task of dragging his cross under the watchful eye of his master, not knowing the reason for his master's request. The second complained of the heaviness of his cross and questioned the motives of his master, imploring his master to shorten his cross. As he traveled on, he asked for his cross to be shortened again, and his master responded to his request. It was only as they traveled on that the two men discovered that their crosses were to be used as a bridge to cross a dangerous river. The shortened cross of the second man could not get him across the river.

This story illustrates that the difficulties we encounter along the way prepare us for greater challenges in the Christian journey. Believers who are accustomed to dragging a heavier cross will be able to use their experience in overcoming difficulties as a bridge to cross over larger flood rivers. The difficulties are often harsh and bitter. The intensity of the suffering that difficulties inflict on us varies from simple to intolerable. We sometimes feel at the limit of our strength and spiritual capacity. Nonetheless, it is important to stand firm, to continue to get rid of our "old man," and, at the same time, to honor our Savior who has preceded us in suffering. Asaph wrote in the Psalms: "If I say, I will speak thus; behold, I should offend against the generation of thy children" (Psalm 73:15). God's children have a way of speaking and behaving—even while beset by difficulties.

Let us take the examples of Elijah (2 Kings 2:11) and of Enoch (Gen. 5:24) who grew within periods of spiritual reversal. Even if their environment was corrupt, it did not stop them from pleasing God. As a reward for their faithfulness, the LORD did not allow them to pass through death. They have preceded us in our journey towards eternal redemption. This divine intervention demonstrates the veracity of Jesus' promises that He will return to earth and take us with Him. We must redouble our efforts to act with courage, even if the work is arduous and the path is exhausting and perilous. According to the apostle Paul, the reward far exceeds the difficulties of the present moment (2 Cor. 4:17). Here are several passages of Scripture for our edification that tell us about the important role of the cross in the life of every Christian: Matthew 10:38; Mark 8:34; Luke 9:23; Luke 14:27; 1 Corinthians 1:17, 18; Galatians 6:12,14; Ephesians 2:16; Philippians 3:18; Hebrews 12:2.

Everyone Has His Cross and Path

Our heavenly Father has a plan of love for each of us to give us eternal life. Because we have not had the same education, nor do we have the same customs, manners, or genetic background, the Lord uses different means to transform us into the image of His Son. The goal of our Father for each of us is the same—to take us through different stages of transformation that we may resemble Christ.

When living as a couple, sometimes one partner can help bear difficulties and worries for the other. Yet, each one has his or her own particular challenges, and our partner may well be incapable of helping us with it, except by prayer. On the other hand, not all believers are at the same level in their spiritual journey. The teacher, the Holy Spirit, cannot teach the same lesson to all His students at the same time. Those who are more advanced must move on to the next lesson, while others are still assimilating the previous lesson. In addition, there are lessons that the Spirit reserves for students who will be called upon to perform special tasks. The experience of the apostle John was different from that of the apostle Peter. John 21:18–22 reports a rather peculiar interview between Jesus and Peter. Jesus gave clues as to how Peter would end his days. At the same time, Peter saw John coming, and Peter asked Jesus what was going to happen to him. Jesus answered: "If I will that he tarry till I come, what is that to thee? follow thou me" (John 12:22). It is clear that Peter and John would have to carry forward the work of the Lord on different paths. Also, one's ability to learn the different lessons is dependent upon one's previous experiences. When we finish one class, having mastered its lessons, we pass the test and go on to the next grade. The Lord's school for the believer is real school with real lessons to learn and real exams to pass. Before Paul's conversion to Christianity, he persecuted Christians. After his conversion, he was persecuted by the Jews. Because of the gospel, he was beaten, humiliated, stoned, and imprisoned.

After his stoning, he continued to fortify the disciples in company with Barnabas. The two exhorted the disciples to persevere in the faith, and declared: "we must through much tribulation enter into the kingdom of God" (Acts 14:22). Difficulties and tribulations are the Christian's cross.

God Transforms Us Through Difficulties

In the verses that follow, the apostle recounts his painful experiences, his humiliations, as well as his spiritual progress. "But in all things approving ourselves as the ministers of God, in much patience, in afflictions, in necessities, in distresses, in stripes, in imprisonments, in tumults, in labours, in watchings, in fastings; by pureness, by knowledge, by longsuffering, by kindness, by the Holy Ghost, by love unfeigned, by the word of truth, by the power of God, by the armour of righteousness on the right hand and on the left, by honour and dishonour, by evil report and good report: as deceivers, and yet true" (2 Cor. 6:4–8). Paul lists in this text many of the difficulties he experienced. These difficulties contributed to the formation of his character.

The Old Testament also abounds in examples of calamities the Lord allowed to come upon His people to make them aware of their evil choices. When a person has abundance, joy, and peace, there is a tendency to act against God's will. The apostle Paul took possession of God's spiritual weapons to confront his problems. He employed prayer, righteousness, faith, the word of God, truth, and sanctification (Eph. 6:13–18). The Holy Spirit uses these means to purify us as the goldsmith passes the gold through the fire to purify it until He can see his own reflection in it. Prayer, fasting, and all the weapons of God are the path that leads to this new life of which the Holy Spirit is the craftsman.

I often have the privilege of speaking with people who are bruised by difficulties. They are a source of inspiration for our spiritual life when they acquire patience, endurance, goodness, humility, discernment, benevolence, and even wisdom. On one occasion, I had a problem, and an experienced pastor had come to pray with me. In his meditation he said that, when a problem happens to us, we are often surprised. However, God is not surprised. In His foreknowledge, He was already aware before the problem arose. If we are His children, we must put the problem back into His hands. For there is no problem that He cannot solve.

> We are troubled on every side, yet not distressed; we are perplexed, but not in despair; persecuted, but not forsaken; cast down, but not destroyed; always bearing about in the body the dying of the Lord Jesus, that the life also of Jesus might be made manifest in our body. For we which live are alway delivered unto death for Jesus' sake, that the life also of Jesus might be made manifest in our mortal flesh. (2 Cor. 4:8–11)

In speaking about the process that leads to the death of the carnal man, Paul made himself the example. Then he described his experience in relation to his knowledge of the Word of God. The difficulties permitted by God allow his "old man" to be constantly delivered to death until he becomes inactive. It is at this moment that the life of Jesus Christ develops and manifests itself in us. The Galatians were Paul's spiritual children. He wanted to see the image of Christ gradually develop in them. After the carnal man has died and the new birth takes place, the Holy Spirit no longer has a barrier in communicating with our spirit and allowing us to be more like Christ. Notice Paul's statement: "My little children, of whom I travail in birth again until Christ be formed in you" (Gal. 4:19). It is evident that the reason our "old man" is delivered to death every day in connection with the death of Jesus is so that the Spirit can reproduce Christ's image in us. The apostle Paul said, "until Christ be formed" in us. Most people agree that Christ is not formed in the believer in a single day. Our Father has put everything in place to make it possible that this change take effect over time. It is a progressive education system. It is more than evident that difficulties are the weapon that God uses through the ministry of the Holy Spirit to produce in us the death of the "old man" and the new birth. Peter wrote: "Beloved, think it not strange concerning the fiery trial which is to try you, as though some strange thing happened unto you: but rejoice, inasmuch as ye are partakers of Christ's sufferings; that, when his glory shall be revealed, ye may be glad also with exceeding joy" (1 Peter 4:12, 13).

I remind you that the key terms, the "old man" (Rom. 6:6), "the flesh" (Rom. 7:5, 25; 8:5), or carnal man, and "members" (Rom. 6:13, 19; 7:5, 23) are all synonymous, and are all the opposite of the "inner man." When we acknowledge our limits and recognize before God our weakness and impotence, when we no longer trust our carnal abilities in decision making and realize our need to consult the Eternal God, this is all proof that we are on the path of spiritual transformation. The process of the destruction of the outer man is underway. It is to our advantage for the external man to be destroyed, even if it requires suffering. Such destruction frees our spirit to become spiritually stronger. "This is why we do not lose courage. Though our outer self is heading for decay, our inner self is being renewed daily" (2 Cor. 4:16, CJB). The inner man, or inner self, refers to the spirit of man. There is a lesson to learn in every occurrence in our lives. We must remain flexible and attentive to grasp the instruction of the Holy Spirit. Knowledge of the word of God and discernment from the Holy Spirit will enable us to distinguish the suggestions of the Holy Spirit from those of evil spirits.

The psalmist David wrote: "You have purified us with fire, O Lord, like silver in a crucible" (Ps. 66:10, TLB). Madame Guyon agreed with David when she said: "It is the fire of suffering that brings forth the gold of godliness." The book of Revelation, which represents a masterpiece of prophecies announcing the imminent return of Jesus, transports us into the realities of the restored earth. The author of the book is the prophet John who was exiled to the island of Patmos for preaching the gospel. We may wonder why God would allow John to be exiled. What we know is that the Lord used John's time of solitude, isolation, and persecution to complete His revelation concerning the plan of redemption.

A Christian, after passing through the molding of the Holy Spirit, is purified like gold and silver in the crucible. It is at this moment that the real Christian life and constant spiritual progression begins. Ours is a living God. He reveals Himself to us to reassure us that we are His children. The carnal side of our nature will take less and less place in our interactions with our fellow men and with the Lord. We will give less importance to the small disturbances of life. Our academic knowledge and our material possessions will be less important to us. We will be better able to forgive those who have offended us. All this will be possible because the Holy Spirit, who is the life of Christ, will dwell in us. "The Spirit itself beareth witness with our spirit, that we are the children of God" (Rom. 8:16).

The Cross is the Path of Glory

"For it is commendable if someone bears up under the pain of unjust suffering because they are conscious of God. But how is it to your credit if you receive a beating for doing wrong and endure it? But if you suffer for doing good and you endure it, this is commendable before God" (1 Peter 2:19, 20, NIV). We saw in the second chapter of the Epistle to the Philippians that God in sovereignty elevated Jesus because He humbled Himself to the point of death on the cross. If we want to be glorified by God, we must serve Him in true humility. It is the cross that gives us access to the kingdom of God. Its role is to destroy our evil traits of character and replace them with virtues. There is no other way that leads to salvation except the way of the cross. "Now if we died with Christ, we believe that we will also live with him" (Rom. 6:8, NIV). The test is that which acts on a person to demonstrate the reality of a person's weaknesses and virtues. It demonstrates how long we can wait, how long we can trust, how long we can endure, bear, forgive, and so on.

Chapter 8
The New Birth

The Greek term for "to be born again" is *gennaō anōthen*, which can also be translated "to be born from above." The birth that comes from above is the new nature that comes from God through the ministry of the Holy Spirit (1 John 3:9).

The new birth is being born a second time, which means that we had already received this same birth at creation. Nonetheless, spiritual death swallowed up this creation after sin. Through the plan of redemption, God has seen fit to give it back to His children. "Blessed be the God and Father of our Lord Jesus Christ, who according to his great mercy hath regenerated us unto a lively hope, by the resurrection of Jesus Christ from the dead" (1 Peter 1:3, Douay Rheims). The verb "regenerate," from the Greek word *gennaō*, means "to be born again." Believers are born again—

> *The birth that comes from above is the new nature that comes from God through the ministry of the Holy Spirit.*

or regenerated—by the word of God (1 Peter 1:23). "Regenerated" is composed of two Greek words: the word *genesis*, meaning "generation," and the word *ana*, meaning "again." Regeneration is the establishment of a new order of things in relation to an older one (Matt. 19:28; Titus 3:5). In this process of renewal, man is the central element. Because God has executed the plan of redemption for the benefit of the human race and not for plants or animals, the human race was the first to be affected by redemption. Any Christian who aspires to tread the soil of the new earth must, during his Christian journey, be born again in relation to the blessings we have received in Jesus Christ (1 Peter 1:3).

> *Any Christian who aspires to tread the soil of the new earth must, during his Christian journey, be born again in relation to the blessings we have received in Jesus Christ*

The Resurrection or the New Birth

Easter is the greatest feast of Christianity, for it is the celebration of the death and resurrection of Jesus. His death is associated with the death of the "old man," and His resurrection is associated with the new birth of each believer—hence the need to remain attached to Him and under His care that our lives may be transformed into His image.

"For whom he did foreknow, he also did predestinate to be conformed to the image of his Son, that he [the Son] might be the firstborn among many brethren" (Rom. 8:29). In Ezekiel 36, God promised to give humans a new heart and a new spirit that they might serve Him. This implies that, when they sinned, humans experienced a certain weakness in their ability to respond favorably to God's desire. In addressing Cain (Gen. 4), the Lord judged that, even after sin, humankind still possessed the ability to choose that which is good. However, observing the failure of the human race and their spiritual resources, which are fading by the day, our Father has made plans to assist us. He wants to give us hearts more fit to serve Him (Ezek. 36). We will consider what the Bible says about the heart later on and whether it is the vital organ that sends blood throughout the body or the very essence of our being, the source of our thoughts, feelings, and cognitive abilities. Yet, first, we should consider Jesus' statement on the new birth.

> There was a man of the Pharisees, named Nicodemus, a ruler of the Jews: the same came to Jesus by night, and said unto him, Rabbi, we know that thou art a teacher come from God: for no man can do these miracles that thou doest, except God be with him. Jesus answered and said unto him, Verily, verily, I say unto thee, Except a man be born again, he cannot see the kingdom of God. Nicodemus saith unto him, How can a man be born when he is old? can he enter the second time into his mother's womb, and be born? Jesus answered, Verily, verily, I say unto thee, Except a man be born of water and of the Spirit, he cannot enter into the kingdom of God. That which is born of the flesh is flesh; and that which is born of the Spirit is spirit. Marvel not that I said unto thee, Ye must be born again. (John 3:1–7)

It is clear that the new birth, which is symbolized by the baptism of water, becomes a reality through the work of the Holy Spirit in destroying the "old man" and reviving the spirit of man in connection with the death and resurrection of Jesus Christ. I do not know if you have already taken time to meditate on this passage, which holds very important information about the new birth. First, we may notice that Jesus Christ made the same declaration twice, using the words, "Verily, verily." The repetition of "verily, verily" (Greek, *amēn, amēn*) demonstrates the importance of this statement for Jesus. Moreover, in verse 7, He added a verb of obligation: "Do not be surprised that I told you, you *must* be born again" (emphasis added). Thus, according to Jesus, to enter the kingdom of God, every person must be born of water and of the Spirit. The rebirth *by water* points to baptism by immersion, which symbolizes that our "old man" accompanied by our past is laid to rest and buried in the water at the moment we go under. We then rise from our watery burial in a new life for the glory of God. Yet, we must understand that this transformation does not happen automatically on the day of baptism. Baptism also symbolizes our consent and our connection with Christ so that the Holy Spirit may apply its corrections in our lives as He annihilates the "old man" and produces the new birth. All people derive their origin from Adam. Since Adam was carnal, all the children of Adam are carnal. "That which is born of the flesh is flesh" (John 3:6a). We are carnal, and "the mind set on the flesh is hostile toward God" (Rom. 8:7, NASB). Therefore, a new spiritual birth is necessary for all people to enter into communion with God, their Father and Lord.

For this reason Jesus declares in verse 6: "That which is born of the flesh is flesh; and that which is born of the Spirit is spirit." As children of Adam, we are carnal. Yet, we become children of God as God sends the Holy Spirit to our spirit's aid by delivering it from the grip of the "old man." Therefore, the first Spirit, which begins with a capital "S," is the Holy Spirit, while the second spirit, which begins with a lower case "s," is the spirit of man. This means that the new birth consists in the rebirth of the spirit of man. In 2 Corinthians 4:16, the apostle Paul encourages us to face difficulties with hope because our inner man is renewed from day to day, while our outer man (our "old man" or carnal nature) is destroyed. He wrote: "Our bodies are dying, our spirits are being renewed every day" (2 Cor. 4:16, NLT). This means that a person's spirit becomes freer and stronger spiritually in proportion to the diminishing of the carnal man. Thus, our bad traits of character gradually disappear in favor of virtues and good qualities. Dr. R. C. Trench calls this the "putting on of the new man, and putting off the old ... This is the gradual conforming of the man more and more to that new spiritual world into which he has been introduced, and in which he now lives and moves" (Richard C. Trench, *Synonyms of the New Testament*, pp. 65, 66). Our life must gradually conform to the life of the new spiritual world created by the plan of redemption. In Galatians 4:19, the apostle Paul expresses an ardent desire to see in the life of the Galatians the gradual implantation of the life they have received from Jesus Christ. He said, "My dear children, for whom I am again in the pains of childbirth until Christ is formed in you" (Gal. 4:19, NIV).

We always like to be in full possession of our means and abilities, to meet our needs without resorting to the help of others. It makes us feel more valuable and increases our pride. Our Lord wants us to have some dependence so we can avoid being proud. Paul was a scholar and a strong man who persecuted the Christians. When the Lord wanted to use Paul, He struck him with blindness. Being blind, Paul was now dependent, having lost his way. In Acts 9, God sent Ananias to lay his hand on Paul so that he could recover his sight. We see in 2 Corinthians 12:7–10 that, despite all his knowledge, Paul had a disability that helped him maintain his humility. The Lord God had willed it to be so: "My grace is sufficient for you, for my power is made perfect in weakness" (2 Cor. 12:9, NIV). Paul agreed with the Lord, saying, "That is why, for Christ's sake, I delight in weaknesses, in insults, in hardships, in persecutions, in difficulties. For when I am weak, then I am strong" (2 Cor. 12:10, NIV). Before Paul's conversion, he was carnally strong. After he had been struck with blindness on the way to Damascus, he was reduced to weakness. All the difficulties that Paul mentions in the text have the role of destroying his carnal man and strengthening his spirit. The Christian must remain calm before difficulties and seek God's help through perseverance in prayer. We are weak when our "old man" becomes impotent before difficulties. However, it is when our "old man" becomes powerless that we allow God, through the Holy Spirit, to take control of our destiny. When the Spirit of God is in control, we are spiritually strong.

Some biblical texts have hidden treasures. If our thinking is not emancipated we cannot communicate with God. Communication is by prayer, meditation, and revelation; and this contact becomes perceptible in our decisions and in our choices. "But we all, with unveiled face, beholding as in a mirror the glory of the Lord, are being transformed into the same image from glory to glory, just as from the Lord, the Spirit" (2 Cor. 3:18). When the outer man is destroyed, according to John 3:6, our spirit is reborn. This is the new birth. Once awakened, the spirit of the person can connect with the Holy Spirit, and the Holy Spirit will allow people to see and understand many things when the veil that shrouded their understanding is taken away.

The Heart

The Greek *kardia*, translated "heart," is the seat of physical life (Acts 14:17; James 5:5), of the moral nature, of the spiritual nature, and of affliction (John 14:1; Rom. 9:2; 2 Cor. 2:4). It is also the seat of joy (John 16:22), of desires (Matt. 5:28), of affections (Luke 24:32), of perceptions (John 12:40), of understanding (Matt. 13:15), of imagination (Luke 1:51), of consciousness (1 John 3:20), of intentions (Heb. 4:12; 2 Cor. 9:7), of the will (Rom. 6:17), and of faith (Mark 11:23). It is where we think (Matt. 9:4) and reason (Mark 2:6, Luke 24:38). The Greek word *psuchē* (life, soul) is translated "heart" in Ephesians 6:6, as "life" and "lives" in 1 John 3:16, and *ek psuchē* is translated "heartily" in Colossians 3:23. All these biblical definitions demonstrate that the heart is not just the organ that pumps blood to our various organs. In the biblical sense, the heart is where thinking takes place. To have a new heart is to receive a new life, to become a new creature. The reason God wanted to give His children a new heart and a new spirit (Ezek. 36:26, 27) is that we might have the capacity to follow the ordinances and practices of God's laws. "For out of the heart proceed evil thoughts, murders, adulteries, fornications, thefts, false witness, blasphemies" (Matt. 15:19). Having a new heart means becoming a new creature by means of the process of regeneration.

A Grafted Creature

Having a new heart means becoming a new creature by means of the process of regeneration.

Our Father has sent Jesus Christ as a second Adam, born of Mary and the Holy Spirit, to defeat Satan and redeem all human beings who accept His salvation. He put everything in place to make us new people, with the perpetual help of the Holy Spirit that we might battle Satan and his forces until the final victory. It is an equation of near equivalency. The Holy Spirit and Mary produce a new Adam in the person of Jesus. We are also called to join the Holy Spirit to form lives in the image of Jesus Christ (1 Cor. 15:45; 2 Cor 5:17). We are in Christ Jesus by the miracle of the Incarnation as, through Him, we live in "heavenly places" (Eph. 2:6). We tend to believe that we are mostly weak creatures, and this is true as it has to do with the life we led before our real conversion. It is faith that can make our conversion effective. I have taken care to add the adjective "real" because conversion does not mean simply being immersed in water and coming out of it. It is a *real* process of change from the life of Adam to that of Jesus, centered on the work of the Holy Spirit in connection with the collaboration of the believer. I am obliged to return to John 3:6. When Nicodemus asked Jesus how an adult could re-enter his mother's womb and be reborn, Jesus replied, in effect: Your first birth was carnal because it came from Adam. I, the Son of God, speak to you and offer you a spiritual birth which comes from above.

A. The human race in Jesus Christ

"You are partners with Christ Jesus because of God. Jesus has become our wisdom sent from God, our righteousness, our holiness, and our ransom from sin" (1 Cor. 1:30, *GOD'S WORD*). To overcome our weakness, which allows Satan to take advantage of us, our heavenly Father will perform many miracles on our behalf through the incarnation, life, death, and resurrection of Jesus Christ. "God sending his own Son in the likeness of sinful flesh, and for sin, condemned sin in the flesh" (Rom. 8:3). So we must understand that the problem lies in our flesh. To overcome, our flesh must be doomed to death (see Rom. 6:6, 7; 7:5, 6; Gal. 6:15). "At that day ye shall know that I am in my Father, and ye in me, and I in you" (John 14:20). Consider verses 10 and 17, considering especially the terms "in me," "in my Father," and "in you." "Believest thou not that I am in the Father, and the Father in me? the words that I speak unto you I speak not of myself: but the Father that dwelleth in me, he doeth the works" (John 14:10). "Even the Spirit of truth; whom the world cannot receive, because it seeth him not, neither knoweth him: but ye know him; for he dwelleth with you, and shall be in you" (John 14:17). Jesus was clothed with human nature. However, since the Father was in Him, the Father acted through Him. We can deduce that Jesus wants to be in us for the same reason—that He may be able to act through us. Our heavenly Father put us in Jesus in the same way that the high priest entered the Most Holy Place with the names of the twelve tribes on his breast, so that he might be able to act on our behalf and so that the repercussions of His actions may give us access to His many divine blessings. "And hath raised us up together, and made us sit together in heavenly places in Christ Jesus" (Eph. 2:6).

B. Jesus Christ in the believers

"I pray that they will all be one, just as you and I are one—as you are in me, Father, and I am in you. And may they be in us so the world will believe you sent me. I have given them the glory you gave me, so they may be one as we are one. I am in them and you are in me. May they experience such perfect unity that the world will know that you sent me and that you love them as much as you love me. I have revealed you to them, and I will continue to do so. Then your love for me will be in them, and I will be in them" (John 17:21–23, 26, NLT). Since our Father in heaven has already done all that is necessary to graft us into Christ, Jesus Christ could describe us as having joined with Him as a single plant, of which He is the vine and we the branches. I remember transplanting a wild branch onto an eggplant stock. The plant produced beautiful, delicious eggplants. Had it not produced fruit, the wild plant would only have served to be ripped from the ground and burned in the fire. Yet, because it was grafted, it became useful. It was no longer a wild plant. It was transformed into a plant capable of producing edible fruit. God does the same thing for us through the work of Jesus Christ and the Holy Spirit. Once the transplant has taken place, our heavenly Father brings it to fruition. The blood of Jesus Christ justifies and purifies us before God. Jesus has also redeemed us by His death, which is symbolically ours. His incarnation and the gift of the Holy Spirit in us are essential elements of the plan of redemption, for they formalize the union between the divine and human natures. This divine-human connection produces a new spiritually stronger person who can face Satan's repeated attacks until the final victory is attained.

A Successful Graft

"For if we have become united with him in the likeness of his death, we shall be also in the likeness of his resurrection; knowing this, that our old man was crucified with him , that the body of sin might be done away, that so we should no longer be in bondage to sin" (Rom. 6:5, 6, ASV). The graft becomes a reality when the "old man" who is the seat of sin has been destroyed, causing sin to lose its residence. Moreover, the new birth has taken place, and the Holy Spirit dwells within us. That is why Paul declared that we form a single plant with Jesus, for the death of the carnal man is the precondition for the new birth. Once this condition has been met, the Holy Spirit has the freedom to establish His dwelling in us. Of course, I am not claiming that the believer was totally deprived of the Spirit's presence before he was born again. In telling us that we have become a single plant with Jesus Christ, Paul is only repeating what Jesus Christ already declared in John 15. Yet, it is important to emphasize that the apostle identified the essential condition for becoming one plant in the resurrection with Jesus Christ. We must die and then come to life in accordance with the death and resurrection of Jesus Christ.

Jesus makes this truth plain in John 15:

> I am the true vine, and My Father is the vinedresser. Every branch in Me that does not bear fruit, He takes away; and every branch that bears fruit, He prunes it so that it may bear more fruit. You are already clean because of the word which I have spoken to you. Abide in Me, and I in you. As the branch cannot bear fruit of itself unless it abides in the vine, so neither can you unless you abide in Me. I am the vine, you are the branches; he who abides in Me and I in him, he bears much fruit, for apart from Me you can do nothing. If anyone does not abide in Me, he is thrown away as a branch and dries up; and they gather them, and cast them into the fire and they are burned. If you abide in Me, and My words abide in you, ask whatever you wish, and it will be done for you. My Father is glorified by this, that you bear much fruit, and so prove to be My

disciples. Just as the Father has loved Me, I have also loved you; abide in My love. (John 15:1–9, NASB)

The analogy about the relationship that must exist between Jesus, who is the vine, and the believers, who are the branches, is striking. The sap that carries nutrition in the plant flows from the vine to the branches. The two parts of the plant are intimately connected. However, if the branches are severed from the vine and its roots, they cannot produce a substitute rootstock. In Jesus' discourse, He emphasized the importance of developing this connection, that is, a close relationship that allows Jesus to express Himself through us. He points out how essential it is that we remain intimately bound to Him that we may bear fruit. Our Father's goal is to see the image of our Elder Brother, Jesus Christ, reflected in us. "For those who He has known beforehand He has also pre-destined to bear the likeness of His Son" (Rom. 8:29, Weymouth). Because Jesus is our brother, it means that we share with Him spiritual characteristics and common rights. Paul did not invent the idea that Jesus is our brother. He took up the words of Jesus Himself. The Gospels of Matthew and John report two statements of the Lord in which He called His disciples "brothers." "Go and tell my brothers to leave for Galilee" (Matt. 28:10, NIV). "Go instead to my brothers and tell them, 'I am ascending to my Father and your Father, to my God and your God'" (John 20:17, NIV). It is not enough to spend but a moment with Jesus and then go away. He said Himself that those who put their hand to the plow and look back are not worthy of Him. Therefore, how we finish our Christian journey is of great importance. We must remain in Him so that His nature permeates us and transforms us day after day until we reflect Christ's image. Only the branches that remain attached to the vine are able to produce good fruit.

Clarification

The apostle Paul revealed in detail the unfolding of the plan of salvation since the establishment of Christianity. He identified the spiritual blessings that attend it and proposed the attitude needed in order to take possession of it. These beneficial tips are the result of his fruitful experience. He particularly acknowledged, in the letter to the Romans, the struggles he had with the "old man" and his inability to make choices in conformity to the will of God. Yet, once he experienced the death of the carnal man and was born again, He said that he was crucified with Christ and became a new creature. If he lives now, it is no longer he who lives but Christ who lives in him. He even asked his readers to imitate him in the same way that he imitated Christ. The spiritual maturity of the believer is acquired through the practice and exercise of the Christian life. We are aware that, as every believer is just beginning the Christian life, he or she can say, "Before I was humbled, I wandered away" (Ps. 119:67a, ISV). Nevertheless, it is necessary to return to the path of salvation and to maintain the course.

If we put the following recommendations into practice, we will see these spiritual realities take place in our lives. Paul counsels us to consider ourselves "dead to sin and alive to God in Christ Jesus" (Rom. 6:11, ESV). In verse 13, he added, "present yourselves to God as those who have been brought from death to life, and your members to God as instruments for righteousness" (Rom. 6:13, ESV). God implores us to offer our "bodies to God as a living sacrifice, holy and pleasing to God" (Rom. 12:1, NIV). It is our responsibility to give ourselves voluntarily to God. We must also see ourselves, accept ourselves, and behave as dead to sin and as living for God. Without this prior step on the part of believers, the Holy Spirit cannot help us progress on the path of the death of the carnal nature. The necessary steps are: looking at oneself as dead to sin, giving ourselves to God as instruments of righteousness, and plunging into the domain of faith. We must believe God and demonstrate our hope in His promises, and then we shall see them fulfilled (Mark 11:24; Heb. 11:1).

Chapter 9
Transformed Christians

Paul wrote in his Ephesian letter: "For ye were sometimes darkness, but now are ye light in the Lord: walk as children of light: (For the fruit of the Spirit is in all goodness and righteousness and truth;)" (Eph. 5:8, 9).

The Fruit of the New Birth
A child who does not eat enough to allow him to absorb the nutrients essential to his development will not have normal growth. His parent or guardian must carefully procure him balanced food until he reaches a certain maturity in his growth and can take charge of his own care. A chronic deficiency of essential nutrients will result in growth problems, and the child will become sickly. Such a situation is very similar to that which believers can experience in their spiritual development. R. C. Trench compares a passive, inactive, disengaged Christian, who does not grow up, to a child who does nothing with his birth. Such a person does not see the need to go to school, to develop all the possibilities and abilities that God has placed in him. Believers must grow spiritually—supporting and forgiving one another—until they come to the unity of the faith.

Do nothing in a spirit of factiousness or of vainglory, but, with true humility, let every one regard the rest as being of more account than himself, each fixing his attention, not simply on his own interests, but on those of others also. Yet the same disposition be in you which was in Christ Jesus. Although from the beginning He had the nature of God He did not reckon His equality with God a treasure to be tightly grasped. Nay, He stripped Himself of His glory, and took on Him the nature of a bondservant by becoming a man like other men. And being recognized as truly human, He humbled Himself and even stooped to die; yes, to die on a cross. It is in consequence of this that God has also so highly exalted Him, and has conferred on Him the Name which is supreme above every other. (Phil. 2:3–9, Weymouth)

Jesus left all the privileges He had with His Father, especially His divine rank, to put on human nature, to experience thirst, hunger, frustration, humiliation, insult, and He did this out of love for us. When Jesus died, Satan thought he had pulled off a great defeat. Yet, Jesus' death was an unequivocal victory that confirmed the fulfillment of His mission and the transfer of spiritual power to every believer through Jesus' death and the outpouring of the Holy Spirit. The apostle Paul advised us not to seek vainglory, but, rather, to follow the example of Jesus Christ—to be animated by Jesus' sentiments of service and humility. Jesus is our great Elder Brother, our ultimate example. We must imitate Him in treading the path of self-denial and humility. It is this path that leads to joy, inner freedom, peace, and eternal glory. After His humiliating death on the cross, He received a new name—"Lord"—which is above all other names. Therefore, it is evident that the path of humility is the only way for any believer to be glorified by God. When the mother of the sons of Zebedee asked Jesus to place, in His kingdom, her two sons—one on His right hand and the other on His left, Jesus told her that this choice was reserved for His Father to make. He also added another interesting point in verse 25. "Jesus called them together and said, 'You know that the rulers of the Gentiles lord it over them, and their high officials exercise authority over them. Not so with you. Instead, whoever wants to become great among you must be your servant, and whoever wants to be first must be your slave—just as the Son of Man did not come to be served, but to serve, and to give his life as a ransom for many'" (Matt. 20:25–28, NIV). And earlier He had said: "Nor are you to be called instructors, for you have one Instructor, the Messiah. The greatest among you will be your servant. For those who exalt themselves will be humbled, and those who humble themselves will be exalted" (Matt. 23:10–12, NIV). Adversity is often beneficial for the Christian. It is more profitable on the spiritual level to be viewed in a negative light, even if we are sincere in our actions, for, it prompts us to seek God in humility and prayer instead of boasting.

"In fact, some parts of the body that seem weakest and least important are actually the most necessary. And the parts we regard as less honorable are those we clothe with the greatest care. So we carefully protect those parts that should not be seen" (1 Cor. 12:22, 23, NLT). If we reflect on all that we do with our hands, we would likely conclude that hands are essential for the proper functioning of the body. In addition to all less honorable jobs they perform, such as helping with personal hygiene and cleaning the house and the yard, they also prepare food, are used to greet people, wield the pen and type the letters in writing beautiful speeches, feed us, and many other things. They serve all the other members of the body, especially those that need the most help and are considered less honorable. Therefore, the weakest members submit to the ministry of the strongest.

"But the fruit of the Spirit is love, joy, peace, patience, kindness, goodness, faithfulness, gentleness, self-control; against such there is no law" (Gal. 5:22, 23, ESV). This list contrasts with behaviors that are contrary to the Christian ethics in verses 19–21. In verse 22, Paul enumerates the fruit of the Spirit. The primary goal of every Christian is to see Jesus Christ face to face on the day of His second advent and receive an eternal crown. The word of God is a mirror. Reading it will allow us to recognize our spiritual state and, with the help of the Holy Spirit, to make the necessary corrections. This work must be gradual while looking at Jesus, the perfect model. The Holy Spirit will guide us because of our desire to progress in our relationship with Jesus Christ. Let us be models, above all, in word and in deed—for our actions are often more eloquent than our words. Benjamin Franklin said: "None preaches better than the ant, and yet she says nothing."

The Christian and Self-control

In general, when a person is insulted, deceived, disappointed, wounded, or upset because of a conflict with someone else or because his temperament clashes with the behavior of another person, that person's natural reaction, as a son of Adam, is to get angry. The entity within him that drives him to anger is called the "carnal man." In Romans 8:7, Paul tells us that the flesh is opposed to God and cannot please Him. James echoed the same thought when he concluded that anger does not fulfill the righteousness of God. "My dear brothers and sisters, take note of this: Everyone should be quick to listen, slow to speak and slow to become angry, because human anger does not produce the righteousness that God desires" (James 1:19, 20, NIV).

We have already explained in Chapter 5 the procedure that God uses, through the work of the Holy Spirit, to solve the problem of the carnal man who prevents us from serving God better. We must understand that the carnal man must diminish for the Spirit to be able to guide us through our minds. This progressive effort of the Spirit, in collaboration with our spirit, will lead us to the progressive acquisition of self-control. "The Spirit, on the other hand, brings a harvest of love, joy, peace; patience towards others, kindness, benevolence, good faith, meekness, self-restraint. Against such things as these there is no law" (Gal. 5:22, 23, Weymouth). "For this very reason, make every effort to supplement your faith with virtue, and virtue with knowledge, and knowledge with self-control, and self-control with steadfastness, and steadfastness with godliness" (2 Peter 1:5, 6, ESV).

We may decide to follow Jesus during a series of lectures or Bible studies. Yet, we often follow Him in ignorance of the rules that Jesus established for His disciples. In Luke 9:23, He gave two unavoidable principles: the disciple must "deny himself, and take up his cross daily, and follow" Jesus. It is not always easy to empty ourselves completely and abandon ourselves to Jesus. Nor is it easy to bear the difficulties symbolized by the cross. Our "old man," who is not dead, occupies a preponderant place in our lives, and our way of interacting with our fellow men shows that it is a reality. Thierry Pasquier wrote: "Each of us manifests an attachment of a different intensity to his self-contemplation. This attachment is felt in the form of more or less intense needs" (*Le Guerrier Intérieur* [The Inner Warrior], pocket edition, p. 117). This is the result of sufficiency, which is the force engendered by the image that people have of themselves. On the other hand, Pasquier says that humility comes from the human ability to detach ourselves from the illusory games of personality, to lose the importance of ourselves. We might add that self-control and humility are virtues that cannot be acquired by human will alone. We will progress only when we strive to collaborate with the Spirit of God in His work of gradual transformation. The natural man does not tend to abandon himself and yield control of himself. It is the troubles of life that are responsible for producing self-denial in us and arousing in us the desire to abandon all else to take refuge in Jesus. This was the case of Paul when he declared: "I am torn between the two: I desire to depart and be with Christ, which is better by far" (Phil. 1:23, NIV). He was ready to die if it could bring him to Jesus. The desire to leave everything to ultimately join Jesus, as he described in 1 Corinthians 15, was very strong.

This chapter is intended to help you understand why the Holy Spirit is sometimes so silent, though His presence is very real in the life of the Christian church, as the servants of God, with spiritual lives transformed in word and deed, promote the good news of the gospel through their labors. This subject is of extreme importance for us Christians, and we must plumb its depths.

Healthy Limbs Form a Healthy Body

"Neither circumcision nor uncircumcision means anything; what counts is the new creation" (Gal. 6:15, NIV). "Therefore if any man be in Christ, he is a new creature: old things are passed away; behold, all things are become new" (2 Cor. 5:17).

Christ's first advent facilitated the establishment of the new covenant, based on spiritual sacrifices. The physical sacrifices were the visible shadows of the things to come. The spiritual sacrifices, being invisible, are more difficult to perform (Rom. 12:1). They represent a more advanced stage of divine revelation in the unfolding of the plan of salvation. The divine requirements for Christians are higher because our Father provides us with more possibilities to accomplish His will (see Ezek. 36:26, 27). In Jesus Christ, God has accomplished everything that is necessary for us to become new creatures. Yet, becoming new creatures requires our obedience and commitment to His Word as the source of our spiritual nourishment. According to Jesus' interview with Nicodemus, in John 3, to be a new creature, we must be born again. In Christianity, the Lord raises the bar of expectation but gives us the means to reach the goal.

> For the creation is eagerly awaiting the revelation of God's children, because the creation has become subject to futility, though not by anything it did. The one who subjected it did so in the certainty that the creation itself would also be set free from corrupting bondage in order to share the glorious freedom of God's children. For we know that all the rest of creation has been groaning with the pains of childbirth up to the present time. However, not only the creation, but we who have the first fruits of the Spirit also

groan inwardly as we eagerly await our adoption, the redemption of our bodies. (Rom. 8:19–23, ISV)

In this text, the apostle addressed all of creation, yet he personified nature as desiring the revelation of the sons of God. The whole of the natural world is tainted and marred, and we breathe its miasma and see it in its helplessness. Paul, who lived his Christian life above the level of most people, was doubtless misunderstood. Even today, some of Paul's writings will require more study. In this statement, he wanted to tell us that the situation was unsustainable and that the birth of a new era was necessary for us to be freed from the slavery of corruption. He seems to be projecting his hope beyond this transitory world, waiting for the complete redemption of our bodies and of the natural world.

Paul's message is deep. He claimed the Corinthians as the product of his ministry and implied that his messages would be imprinted in their hearts and characters. He specified that their transformation is the work of the Holy Spirit. He wished that each of us might be a letter of Christ written by the Holy Spirit so that, whenever people meet us—at church or at work, at home or away—they will have an opportunity to discover Christ through us. "You are our letter, written in our hearts, known and read of all men; being manifested that you are a letter of Christ, cared for by us, written not with ink but with the Spirit of the living God, not on tablets of stone but on tablets of human hearts" (2 Cor. 3:2, 3, NAS). These verses invite us to self-evaluation that we might have a more productive Christian experience. It is undeniable that people we meet are reading us every day. What kinds of messages do we project? Do our messages repel or do they attract? Are they inspired by the Holy Spirit or by the personality of our natural man? Whatever the answer, our Father wants us to communicate inspiring messages, honoring and representing Him.

According to the first five verses of First Peter, chapter 2, Jesus Christ wants to build His church with living stones that are rejected by men but chosen and precious to God. Each stone is cut before being integrated into the construction so that it fits well with the other stones that are already cut. To achieve this, a large iron sledgehammer is usually used. Its considerable size increases its impact when it strikes. When the stones were well cut and properly assembled, it was a pleasure to view the masterpiece of construction. Were it not for careful planning and construction, the building could be ugly and prone to collapse. This comparison fits well with the reality of the church. This is why Paul said, "like a wise master builder I laid a foundation, and another is building on it" (1 Cor. 3:10). He understood the importance of a building having a good foundation and a solid structure (see 1 Peter 2:1–5).

Living as Christian Priests

The Hebrew verb translated "consecrate" is *qadas*. "Consecrate" means "to set something or someone apart for a specific task." When applied to the service of God, it means "to set aside," "sanctify," or "make holy someone or something for God's use." In Hebrews 10:20, the meaning of the verb "consecrate" is somewhat qualified. The verb "to consecrate" translates the Greek word *enkainiz* —*en*, meaning "in," and *kainos*, which means "new." It means "inaugurating," or "opening." Through His blood, Jesus *consecrated* to us a new and living way through the veil of His flesh into the holy places in the presence of God. The key that opens the door into God's presence is first the blood of Jesus Christ, then consecration, and then sanctification in prayer.

A priest is called to live in the presence of God. He must live to obey God since the purpose of his consecration is to serve God. To approach God, he must sanctify himself. For this to be possible, he must passionately love his work because his role is to live in the presence of God. Among students who have chosen the same course of study with the same teachers, it is those that develop a passion for their professions who will stand out and excel in their field of expertise. The same holds true for the Christian in the Christian journey.

To avoid dying, the priests had to cleanse themselves with water before entering the presence of God (Exod. 30:20, 21). God's presence becomes an irresistible taste. The one who tastes it does not want to stop. This is how it was with Moses, who wanted the presence of God with all his being. He was privileged to speak verbally to God as He hid Himself in the cloud, meeting with God forty days and forty nights on Mount Sinai. However, this was not enough for him. His attraction to the presence of the Lord prompted him to ask, "Please let me see your glory" (Exod. 33:18, *GOD'S WORD*). Their friendship was so great, that the Lord chose to fulfill Moses' request.

> I will let my goodness pass in front of you, and there I will call out my name 'the LORD.'...But you can't see my face, because no one may see me and live....Stand by this rocky cliff. When my glory passes by, I will put you in a crevice in the cliff and cover

you with my hand until I have passed by. Then I will take my hand away, and you'll see my back, but my face must not be seen. (Exod. 33:19–22, *GOD'S WORD*)

Our satisfaction should not stop because our Father has responded to our requests for help in providing our basic needs of clothes, shelter, and food. There must be a moment when nothing else interests us but the presence of our Father. When our Father sees that we are burning with the desire to meet Him, I assure you, He will come to meet us, for "love begets love" (*The Desire of Ages*, p. 519). At that moment, we can jump into His arms and enjoy His inexpressible love. It is the same with God. He does not hide from those who seek Him. There are experiences that belong only to thirsty people. Revelation 1:6 relates that Jesus made us "priests unto God." Such an identification implies that conditions exist for all Christians to consecrate and sanctify themselves to be able to present themselves personally before God. The white garment which the faithful Witness advises us to buy represents not only justification, which is the imputed righteousness of Christ and a providential measure intended to cover our moral nakedness and sin, but also the next complementary step, which is sanctification, or God's righteousness imparted. Sanctification is the gradual transformation of character in Christian growth and progress during the fight against weaknesses and imperfections through continual victory over sin (see Fernando Chaij, *Preparation for the Final Crisis*, pp. 44–46).

> *Unity and collaboration among all the members who form the body of Christ are paramount to its proper functioning.*

A Person with the Perfect Stature of Christ

"And he gave some, apostles; and some, prophets; and some, evangelists; and some, pastors and teachers; for the perfecting of the saints, for the work of the ministry, for the edifying of the body of Christ: till we all come in the unity of the faith, and of the knowledge of the Son of God, unto a perfect man, unto the measure of the stature of the fulness of Christ" (Eph. 4:11–13).

In verse 13, the apostle expresses the importance of the proper functioning of the body of Christ in order and harmony. Unity and collaboration among all the members who form the body of Christ are paramount to its proper functioning. Unity in love is part of the very nature of God, otherwise the Holy Spirit is saddened and unable to do His work in the body. The talents that each one receives are to contribute to the work of God and the edification of the body of Christ. Everyone must have the same concern—the unity of the church and the spiritual progress of the Lord's work. This should be made manifest in a spirit of service and humility. The arm must obey the head that is Christ, and the hand must work in coordination with the arm. It is the same with all the other members of the body, which also act under the control of the head. It is in this sense that Paul wants us to be people who can operate in the perfect image of the body of Jesus Christ, the church, that our Lord may glorify and honor us.

"For we were all baptized by one Spirit so as to form one body—whether Jews or Gentiles, slave or free—and we were all given the one Spirit to drink" (1 Cor. 12:13, NIV). If we have drunk of the same drink of the Holy Spirit, then we should undergo the same influence and the same transformation. Jesus said that the people of the world occupy positions to dominate others, but, in His kingdom, the rules are different. The governor occupies his position for the purpose of serving (Matt. 20:25–27). The "perfect man," in Ephesians 4:13, describes the church, which is the body of Christ. For the man of perfect stature in Christ to be a reality, each member must fulfill his or her function in harmony with the principles for operation within the body. The man will be the building previously mentioned, built with carefully cut stones, to the Master's approval. The apostle presents us with an image of profound spiritual unity under the guidance of the Holy Spirit. To get some idea of our strengths and weaknesses, all one has to do is compare the ideal with what we actually have in our Christian communities.

> *For the man of perfect stature in Christ to be a reality, each member must fulfill his or her function in harmony with the principles for operation within the body.*

Chapter 10
The Baptism of the Holy Spirit

Jesus told His disciples, "Nevertheless I tell you the truth; It is expedient for you that I go away: for if I go not away, the Comforter will not come unto you; but if I depart, I will send him unto you....Howbeit when he, the Spirit of truth, is come, he will guide you into all truth..." (John 16:7, 13). Understanding the role of the Holy Spirit is essential.

The Holy Spirit in the Life of the Christian

For the next step in the journey, we will need to speak briefly about the Holy Spirit. The subject of the Holy Spirit is complex because the Holy Spirit is God, and God is only known when He reveals a part of Himself to humanity. Maintaining fuzzy ideas about the Holy Spirit is not beneficial, for every Christian needs to understand the role the Holy Spirit plays in the lives of believers. Our spiritual development and Christian experience depend upon the work of the Holy Spirit in our lives. To write this chapter, in addition to reading the biblical data, I take into account my own personal experiences. Jesus said:

And I will pray the Father, and he shall give you another Comforter, that he may abide with you for ever; even the Spirit of truth; whom the world cannot receive, because it seeth him not, neither knoweth him: but ye know him; for he dwelleth with you, and shall be in you. I will not leave you comfortless: I will come to you. Yet a little while, and the world seeth me no more; but ye see me: because I live, ye shall live also. At that day ye shall know that I am in my Father, and ye in me, and I in you. ... And I have declared unto them thy name, and will declare it: that the love wherewith thou hast loved me may be in them, and I in them. (John 14:16–20; 17:26)

This statement reminds us that Jesus promised the Holy Spirit to all who accept Him as Savior and Lord. Without the presence of the Spirit of God, the believer cannot develop or grow in the Christian life. Paul reported in 2 Corinthians: "Now he that stablisheth us with you in Christ, and anointed us, is God; who also sealed us, and gave us the earnest of the Spirit in our hearts" (2 Cor. 1:22, ERV). The Holy Spirit not only marks the believer as God's property, but He is also an "earnest" or guarantee for the believer (see also 2 Cor. 5:5; Eph. 1:14), an asset in anticipation of eternal life.

It is significant to note that the word "in"—in the phrases, "in me," "in them," and "in my Father"—is the Greek word *eis*, which is the preposition "into." However, to avoid dissonance, the French and the English translations use "in" rather than "into." However, the French prepositions *en* ("in") and *dans* ("into") may have very different meanings in sentences such as "I am *into* running," "I am going *on* a trip," "You are traveling *in* advance of me," and so on. The easiest translation in English is "in," which more faithfully translates the thought of God and the idea of the text than "into."

The Holy Spirit is God. God is normally invisible to human eyes, though He uses various means to reveal Himself and manifest His presence to us. He has revealed Himself in angelic form or in human form, as when Abraham "saw three men" (Gen. 18:2). Because this chapter contains very amazing information, I suggest that you read it again.

The LORD performs wonders and miracles through His servants. He verbally delivers orders (as He did to Moses), and He verbally expresses His love (as He did through Jesus). Miraculously He sent Jesus Christ to live among men (John 1:14) and further reveal the character of God (John 1:18; 17:4). After His resurrection, Jesus took care to make several appearances to His followers that they might know that He was really resurrected. When God makes us a promise, He seeks to demonstrate the concrete fulfillment of His promise to us who live in a sensible world. Because Jesus promised His followers the Holy Spirit, the advent of the Holy Spirit had to be perceptible to the eyes of those who received Him (in visible flames of fire in Acts 2:3; cf. in the form of a dove in Matt. 3:16; Mark 1:10; Luke 3:22; John 1:32). Otherwise, their detractors would take the advantage, inventing all kinds of subterfuges to discredit the Spirit's arrival.

The Seal of God on the Christian

A seal certifies the ownership and validity of the document on which it is affixed. It can also be a mark impressed upon a letter to seal it (Rev. 5:1, 2, 5, 9). Paul wrote in Romans: "Anyone who does not have the Spirit of Christ does not belong to him" (Rom. 8:9, ESV). The presence of the Holy Spirit in the life of the believer marks those who are God's children. In Second Timothy, the apostle Paul gave a very revealing definition of the seal: "But God's firm foundation stands, bearing this seal: 'The Lord knows those who are his,' and, 'Let everyone who names the name of the Lord depart from iniquity'" (2 Tim. 2:19). In many places in the world, people brand their animals with seals bearing their initials to mark them as their property. The Lord, in addition to all this, wants to guarantee us, by the Holy Spirit, that He will give us eternal life, as Paul said in Ephesians: "You, too, have heard the word of truth, the gospel of your salvation. When you believed in the Messiah, you were sealed with the promised Holy Spirit, who is the guarantee of our inheritance until God redeems his own possession for his praise and glory" (Eph. 1:13, 14, ISV). The word "guarantee" ("earnest," KJV) comes from the Greek *arrhab n*, and, in modern Greek, *arrhabōna* means "engagement ring." Generally, an engagement predicts that marriage is near. Jesus betrothed a pretty young girl, the church, who is enthusiastically preparing to be even more beautiful on her wedding day, that is, at the return of Jesus Christ. Paul wrote: "Now He who establishes us with you in Christ and anointed us is God, who also sealed us and gave us the Spirit in our hearts as a pledge" (1 Cor. 1:21, 22, NASB). With the contract He has signed, the Lord has given us an advance of funds as a pledge of guarantee that, upon His return, He will finalize the contract and honor His promise. A down payment in hand is confirmation that Jesus will come back to finalize His contract. The image of an engagement ring on the finger is a guarantee that the groom will return at the time set for the nuptial ceremony.

Regarding the Holy Spirit, we can easily entertain vague ideas about His nature, because His presence is not always evident. As an analogy, I would like to draw from my training in electrical engineering and electronics. In training for engineering, I studied the production and transport of thousands of megawatts of voltage. Occasionally, as a technician, I received a shock when I repaired electronic equipment. Knowing firsthand what this sensation feels like, I can imagine the violence of the tremors that one would feel under a stronger current. The same thing is true for a person who has ever had a seizure when an intense fever has spiked. Those who have never had a febrile seizure cannot imagine the sensation that the person who has had one has felt. Yet, just because you may never have had such a febrile experience does not mean that such a thing does not exist, because the symptoms are obvious in the person who has suffered from them. The electric current also exists in reality because its results are real—it turns the fan and makes the light bulb glow. The same is true with the Holy Spirit. His reality is seen in results that are real. The people who are baptized frequently have an unforgettable experience enabling them to grow in their understanding and practice of the Christian life.

> *The Lord has given us an advance of funds as a pledge of guarantee that, upon His return, He will finalize the contract and honor His promise.*

Without the holiness of sanctification, no one can approach God (Heb. 12:14). The high priest was required to sanctify himself carefully before entering the presence of God in the Most Holy Place. It was the same for Moses, who had to sanctify himself to approach God. At one point, the Lord gave Moses an appointment at Mount Sinai. God wanted the people to accompany Moses so that they might be eyewitnesses to the meeting. The Lord had commanded that the people be sanctified for three days, even though they would be following Moses' encounter with God from a distance (Exod. 19). Their cleansing with water illustrates how sanctification is preparatory to the baptism of the Holy Spirit. Whenever needed, the Lord can arouse situations in the lives of His children to destroy the power of the carnal man and put them in a spirit of helplessness and total dependence. In this way, He can create conditions favorable to the baptism of the Holy Spirit.

The Holy Spirit is a living person. In our experiences in the Christian life, it is to our advantage that we sanctify ourselves, leading a life of personal consecration through prayer and centered on God's word and humility. In order to experience the baptism of the Holy Spirit, it is not good to spend our whole life in the courtyard without taking the opportunity to clothe ourselves in sacerdotal garments to enter the Most Holy Place, that is to say, to approach God through the experience of the baptism of the Holy Spirit. As Jesus said to Nicodemus, one cannot enter the kingdom of God without receiving the baptism of the Holy Spirit. I believe that this same recommendation is also addressed to those of us who live at the end of time.

The Baptism of the Holy Spirit

In the 1980s, I had a co-worker with a background in administration. He often repeated that knowledge is power, for it makes it possible to prevent problems and anticipate and make informed decisions. The LORD declared that His "people are destroyed for lack of knowledge" (Hosea 4:6). When we analyze certain experiences of the children of Israel in the Old Testament, we can imagine that, had they been alert, they could have repented to avoid certain disastrous consequences, such as deportation, which arose from their bad choices. Sometimes I have been caught in a difficult situation that required a certain spiritual approach to resolve it. I reacted in an awkward way because I lacked spiritual information that could have changed my attitude in the face of the situation. As a result, the problem remained and even got worse, and the consequences became more serious. On the other hand, when it comes to the Bible, I always try to get closer to the truth to grasp it, if possible. It is true that what matters most is that we develop and maintain a good relationship with Jesus Christ. Yet it is equally important that we understand what He wants to tell us through His Word. If I do not understand what He is saying, I might go left when He is asking me to go right.

The relation of the word "baptism" to other terms in the Bible gives different nuances of meaning, depending on the context of its use. All new believers must be baptized in the name of the Father, the Son, and the Holy Spirit in accordance with the recommendation of Jesus Christ to His disciples in Matthew 28. The believer who is baptized in the name of Jesus Christ, after making a sincere and public commitment, receives the Holy Spirit according to the promise of Jesus. It is also true that the Holy Spirit has to work in the life of the believer to produce the new birth. He is given authority to carry out His ministry on the basis of this public commitment (John 3:6). Therefore, through baptism, we give God the right of ownership over us by covenant. There is another very significant New Testament theme—baptizing into the death of Jesus. This is included being baptized in His name. The officiants always repeat to the one being baptized: "I baptize you in the name of the Father, the Son, and the Holy Spirit." When one is immersed in water, it means that one is immersed, or buried, with our "old man" who is destined to be destroyed. Being baptized into the death of Jesus Christ means that the believer's "old man" must die in conformity to the death of Jesus Christ. Paul wrote: "Buried with him in baptism, wherein also ye are risen with him through the faith of the operation of God, who hath raised him from the dead" (Col. 2:12).

The concept of being baptized by the Holy Spirit (see Matt. 3:16; Luke 3:16; 1 Cor. 12:13) comes from John the Baptist and was taken up by other apostles, including Paul. This concept refers mainly to the outpouring of the Holy Spirit on the day of Pentecost (Acts 2). To understand its meaning, let us analyze the events that occurred on that day. The disciples had already received the Holy Spirit, for John reports that Jesus said: "Peace be unto you: as my Father hath sent me, even so send I you. And when he had said this, he breathed on them, and saith unto them, Receive ye the Holy Ghost" (John 20:21, 22). On this earlier occasion, the concept of the baptism of the Holy Spirit was not mentioned. This would indicate that the baptism of the Holy Spirit is a remarkable and unique manifestation of the Holy Spirit, as was the case at the festival of Pentecost.

This would indicate that the baptism of the Holy Spirit is a remarkable and unique manifestation of the Holy Spirit, as was the case at the festival of Pentecost.

> On the day of Pentecost all the believers were meeting together in one place. Suddenly, there was a sound from heaven like the roaring of a mighty windstorm, and it filled the house where they were

sitting. Then, what looked like flames or tongues of fire appeared and settled on each of them. And everyone present was filled with the Holy Spirit and began speaking in other languages, as the Holy Spirit gave them this ability. At that time there were devout Jews from every nation living in Jerusalem. When they heard the loud noise, everyone came running, and they were bewildered to hear their own languages being spoken by the believers. They were completely amazed. "How can this be?" they exclaimed. "These people are all from Galilee, and yet we hear them speaking in our own native languages!" (Acts 2:1–8, NLT)

Pentecost was an inaugural day—the day that the Holy Spirit became available to all believers. It was a visible manifestation of the Holy Spirit on believers. The Old Testament abounds with examples of the anointing of the Holy Spirit similar to that of Pentecost, though on an individual level. We must understand that "baptism" is a word that belongs to Christianity. It is a step in the unfolding of the plan of salvation. John the Baptist had begun to baptize under the inspiration of the Holy Spirit. Jesus set the example for all His followers by being baptized. Then, before He ascended to heaven, He gave His disciples for all ages the mission of going throughout the world to preach the good news. Then, those who believe were to be baptized in the name of the Father, the Son, and the Holy Spirit (Matt. 28:18–20). The baptism of the Holy Spirit enables the believer to have a clearer idea of the Holy Spirit's person, His presence, and His work. If the Holy Spirit were a totally silent person, it would be difficult for the believer to speak of Him convincingly. Baptism not only aims to fortify us spiritually, but it demonstrates the truth of Jesus' promise. It also represents a wonderful experience in the life of the believer. It may also encourage the believer to come closer to the throne of grace, as is stated about Jesus Christ (Heb. 4:16).

Some people believe that it is easy to receive the Holy Spirit by the laying on of hands, as sometimes happened in the days of the apostles. I am not totally against this way of thinking, since examples of this are found in the sacred writings. Yet, I imagine that, if I lead a spiritual life that is not in accordance with the will of God, the placing of hands on me or on my head cannot have the desired result. I would advise anyone who would like to experience the power of the Holy Spirit and lead an active and engaged Christian life to seek God through prayer and fasting in sanctification. This is the safest way to get there. The baptism of water and the baptism of the Holy Spirit were complementary experiences during

Chapter 10 *The Baptism of the Holy Spirit*

the time of the apostles. Even today, they should be because, without the latter experience, the believer is merely engaging in imaginary swimming (Acts 19:1–6).

We are unanimous in believing that there is one Creator God in three persons: the Father, the Son, and the Holy Spirit. These three persons are intimately connected in a perfect unity. The presence of Jesus is the presence of God (John 14:9). The presence of the Holy Spirit is the presence of God. A sin against the Holy Spirit is a sin against God. The first verse of the Bible clearly expresses this idea. There the word "God" is translated from the Hebrew name *Elohim*, which a plural form. Nonetheless, the verb "created" is not plural but singular. Thus, God manifests Himself in three persons as He carries out the plan of salvation for humankind. First, the Bible presents the Holy Spirit as the Spirit of God. We can verify this in the several scriptures (Gen. 1:2; 41:38; Exod. 31:3; 35:31; Num. 24:2; Judges 3:10; 11:29; 13:25; 14:19; 1 Sam. 10:10; 11:6; 16:13, 14; 19:23; 2 Sam. 23:2; 1 Kings 18:12; 22:24; 2 Kings 2:16; 2 Chron. 18:23; 24:20; Isa. 11:2; 40:13; 59:19; 63:14; Matt. 3:16; 10:20; 12:28; Luke 4:18; Acts 2:17; 8:39; 16:7; Rom. 8:9).

The prophet Joel, in chapter 2, verse 28, prophesied that the Holy Spirit was going to poured out according to the promise of Jesus Christ. This prophecy was taken up in Acts 2:17. There are other texts announcing the baptism of the Holy Spirit (Matt. 3:11; Mark 1:8; Luke 3:16; John 1:33; Acts 1:5). It is important to distinguish between texts that announce the baptism of the Holy Spirit and those that describe the experience proceeding from this baptism. Let us note some texts that highlight the baptism of the Holy Spirit (Luke 1:41, 42, 67–69, Acts 2:4; 4:8, 31; 9:17; 13:9; Luke 3:22; Acts 10:44; 11:15; 19:6). Acts 2:4, which describes Pentecost, is the main text in which the baptism of the Holy Spirit took place in a grand way. Acts 19:1–6 clearly shows that the baptism of the Holy Spirit is a remarkable and unique presence in which beneficiaries, even if unaware of the fact, do not have control over their actions during the time they are filled. Acts 2:4 tells us that the people who were filled with the Holy Spirit spoke as the Spirit gave them utterance. One would assume that the Holy Spirit brought the person into a kind of ecstasy, taking full control of his mind. Therefore, when the person is filled with the Holy Spirit, he or she reacts spontaneously by an action that glorifies God.

I speak about this from personal experience and from observation. During a week of prayer in a Seventh-day Adventist church I witnessed the manifestation of the Spirit, which we can call the baptism of the Holy

Spirit, in a lady who was about fifty years old. In some Old Testament texts, people speak of the Spirit as seizing them or as making them do a certain action. Such descriptions indicate that such persons did not have control of their actions while being filled with the Holy Spirit. May the Holy Spirit accompany every reader seeking to enter into communion with Him.

The Holy Spirit before Baptism

"While Peter still speaking these words, the Holy Spirit fell upon all who were listening to the message. All the circumcised believers who came with Peter were amazed, because the gift of the Holy Spirit had been poured out on the Gentiles also. For they were hearing them speaking with tongues and exalting God. Then Peter answered, 'Surely no one can refuse the water for these to be baptized who have received the Holy Spirit just as we did, can he?'" (Acts 10:44–47, NASB). In this example, we see pagans who have believed in God in their hearts receiving the Holy Spirit even before they are baptized. Thus, we can deduce that the attainment of the Holy Spirit can precede baptism. It is enough to have faith in God and to make the decision to follow Jesus in sincerity. This is the meaning of John 17, verse 26, which says that, when the love of God is in us, Jesus can be in us in the person of the Holy Spirit. We accept that baptism is a sacred symbol, sealed by God, yet the sincerity of the believer's heart plays a crucial role in the free flow of the power of the Holy Spirit. This explains why believers can receive the Holy Spirit before baptism, while others seem not to receive it even after being baptized. God wants to arouse our will, and He wants to see in us evidence that we desire to walk with and pursue Him.

The Holy Spirit and the Prophets

As we mentioned above, there are many examples of the anointing of the Holy Spirit in the Old Testament. Ezekiel relates that, after God addressed him, "the Spirit entered into me and set me on my feet" (Ezek. 2:2, ESV). The records of Chronicles and Samuel declare: "Then in the midst of the assembly the Spirit of the LORD came upon Jahaziel" (2 Chron. 20:14, NASB) and "the Spirit of God came upon the messengers of Saul, and they also prophesied" (1 Sam. 19:20, ESV). Three times the Spirit of God seized Samson at Ashkelon and Lehi, enabling him to bare-handedly tear the lion and the enemies of God (Judges 14:6–9, 19; 15:14–19). Micah cried out that he was filled with the Spirit of the Lord (Micah 3:8). The manner in which the Holy Spirit intervened in certain cases in the Old Testament is comparable to certain aspects of Pentecost.

The person who has the experience of receiving the Holy Spirit knows the experience first hand, feeling it strongly, while others, who have not had the experience, can see its manifestation.

The Roles of the Holy Spirit

"And when he is come, he will reprove the world of sin, and of righteousness, and of judgment: of sin, because they believe not on me; of righteousness, because I go to my Father, and ye see me no more; of judgment, because the prince of this world is judged. I have yet many things to say unto you, but ye cannot bear them now. Howbeit when he, the Spirit of truth, is come, he will guide you into all truth: for he shall not speak of himself; but whatsoever he shall hear, that shall he speak: and he will shew you things to come. He shall glorify me: for he shall receive of mine, and shall shew it unto you" (John 16:8–14).

The functions of the Holy Spirit are many. Without the Holy Spirit, we are unaware of our sinful state and are incapable of practicing justice or understanding that we will be called to judgment for our secret and public actions. His most important function is in transforming the lives of believers to become born-again Christians who lead a fruitful spiritual life in relation to the life of Jesus Christ. In Ephesians 4:30, Paul says, "And do not grieve the Holy Spirit of God, by whom you were sealed for the day of redemption."

Why We Should Not Grieve the Holy Spirit

When the Holy Spirit is grieved by our unpleasant behavior, He ceases His activities in us, except to convince us of sin. As a result, we will become weak and spiritually poor. To live an authentic Christian life, we must have an authentic character that is natural, true, sincere, and just. Some preachers frequently flatter us with messages centered on grace. It is undeniable that we are saved by grace as the means of redemption. Yet, after being saved from a world devoted to perdition (John 12:31), the believer must follow the divine prescriptions to keep himself in God's will and the path that leads to eternal life and the New Jerusalem.

This was the situation for the Jewish people in the desert. They were to obey the Lord's directions to enter Canaan. I invite you to read carefully chapters 4 and 5 of the Epistles to the Ephesians. The first part of chapter 4 speaks about the unity of faith. The unity of faith refers to unity in belief under the influence of the Holy Spirit. Believing in the same truths can give us a common vision of eternal things and develop in us the feelings of respect, solidarity, and mutual support. Verses 11–13 reveal the relational quality that the Lord claims from His children. Some gifts help to repair broken bonds, others to rectify desperate situations, and still others to edify the body of Christ.

The Sadness of the Holy Spirit

Let us return to an important text—Ephesians 4:30—which reveals the reaction of the Holy Spirit to our reprehensible behavior. This text provides us with two important pieces of information: the Holy Spirit can be saddened because of our bad behavior, and we have been sealed by the Holy Spirit for the day of redemption. Therefore, Jesus gives us the Holy Spirit to dwell in us and to accompany us in our spiritual development in anticipation of the day of redemption. Conversely, it is important to know the behavior the Holy Spirit adopts when He is saddened as well as the implications of His sadness in the life of the believer who needs the benefit of the Holy Spirit's active presence.

Paul enumerates for us, in Ephesians 4:17–5:21, a list of sins that sadden the Holy Spirit. From this list we would like to mention the subtlest and most dangerous. Because they seem insignificant, they easily integrate into our routine of life, and society tends to accept them. Yet, the rules of God's holiness are immutable. The holiness of God is opposed to sin. "Without holiness no one will see the Lord" (Heb. 12:14, NIV). The Holy Spirit is God because of the unity of the Godhead, so it is possible to sin against Him. The apostle warns us against impurity, deceitful covetousness, lying to one's neighbor, evil words, bitterness, animosity, slander, wickedness, insults, dishonest words, foolish remarks, jests, and anything contrary to propriety. These all sadden the Holy Spirit.

No one can say that they have ever seen the Holy Spirit, much less a sad look on His face. However, we can perceive and feel the Holy Spirit's action. Our spiritual lethargy can lead us to conclude that we need to sanctify ourselves and clothe ourselves with the power of the Holy Spirit. If we notice that the carnal side of our soul takes greater control of our decisions and our actions, we can deduce that the Holy Spirit is saddened. When He is sad, He remains inactive, yet He continues to convict us about our situation. The Bible indicates that the Holy Spirit can flee from us in the case of blasphemy or outrage (Luke 12:10; Heb. 10:29). These two words have very close meanings in French as in Greek—insult, offense, and outrage. Such implies that blaspheming the Holy Spirit is also an outrage. The apostle John, in Revelation 21:8, mentions a list of human behaviors that displease God. We can imagine that they also sadden the Holy Spirit. Paul suggested other attitudes to avoid to remain in harmony with the Holy Spirit (2 Tim. 3:2–4; Rom. 1:29–31). The Holy Spirit is a divine power that enables us to testify for God in acts and words, in accordance with His will (Acts 1:8). Once He is saddened, we become inactive and ineffective. To have a clearer idea of what it means to sadden the Holy Spirit, let me bring you the testimony of a malefactor, recounted after his conversion.

This converted former malefactor described how he had planned to clandestinely kidnap a child whose mother was a Christian. The day he had designated for executing his plan came. While the child was outside his home, playing with other neighborhood children, the man, in his evil scheme, crept up above the children to nab the child. Yet, he held back from his mission when he saw two angels dressed in soldiers' clothing watching over the child. Because of their presence, he delayed a few minutes. Then, a dispute broke out between the children. The angels were saddened, and they left, and the evildoer seized the child and took him to his house. The Lord in His mercy was going to impress the mother, through the Holy Spirit, to seek her suddenly missing child. Instead, directed the maid in the house where the child was taken to take him back home. The story ended well. However, if two angels (like the Holy Spirit) can be saddened by a dispute among children, much more will they be saddened by disputes among adults. The grieving of heavenly agents should be a source of reflection for us as believers. We need to pay attention to how we react to conflict situations, which are profitable for neither party involved—either for the one who is wrong or for the one who holds a grudge.

Reasons for His Sadness

For the Creator, names are of particular importance. He presented himself in specific circumstances with names that reveal particular aspects of His character in connection with His interventions (e.g., Isa. 9:6; 1 Kings 18:32; 2 Sam. 7:26; Gen. 17:1; Jer. 23:6). It is the same with the Holy Spirit who takes different names in connection with the various aspects of His work. The Lord changed the name of Abram to Abraham so He could bless him and change his destiny. "Neither shall thy name any more be called Abram, but thy name shall be Abraham [Father of a great multitude]; for a father of many nations have I made thee" (Gen. 17:5). He changed the name of Jacob into Israel. "Then he [the Angel] said, 'Your name shall no longer be called Jacob, but Israel, for you have striven with God and with men, and have prevailed'" (Gen. 32:28, 29). Jesus also changed the name of Simon to Peter. "He brought him to Jesus. Jesus looked at him and said, 'You are Simon the son of John. You shall be called Cephas' (which means Peter)" (John 1:42, ESV).

A. Compelling Facts

René Pache did a tremendous job in his book, *The Person and Work of the Holy Spirit*, (pp. 104 and 105). In the paragraph that follows, I will use some of his explanations to highlight behaviors that sadden the Holy Spirit. In chapter 11, verse 2, Isaiah prophesied about the coming of Jesus who will be filled with the Spirit in all its fullness. These characteristics do not mean that there are several Spirits. It is one and the same Spirit with unlimited virtues.

According to Ephesians 5:3, all impurity and all defilement sadden the Holy Spirit, for He is the "Spirit of holiness" (Rom. 1:4). When we ignore spiritual truths, we have little zeal for reading and studying the Bible. The obscurity of the teaching of men distresses Him, for He is the Spirit of revelation, wisdom, understanding, and knowledge (Isa. 11:2; Eph. 1:17; Eph. 5:11–18). All falsehood, all willful inaccuracy, all heresy, all deceitfulness—including the appearance of deceitfulness—and all hypocrisy (Rom. 1:18, Eph. 4:25, 29, 31, Eph. 5:2, 4) sadden Him, for He is the Spirit of truth (John 14:17). All our doubts, discouragements, and nagging questions afflict Him, for He is the Spirit of faith (2 Cor. 4:13). All that is carnal and earthly in our hearts (Rom. 1:28–32) concern Him, for He is the Spirit of glory (1 Peter 4:14). Spiritual weakness, death, and lack of inner development and spiritual power pain Him, for He is the Spirit of strength and life and power (Rom. 8:2; 2 Tim. 1:7, Acts 1:8). Our refusal to forgive, the hardness of our hearts, our indifference to the suffering and perdition of souls, and our lukewarmness towards God sadden Him, for He is the Spirit of love and grace (2 Tim. 1:7; Heb. 10:29). We could add other examples to further crystallize what our spiritual reality should be, yet these examples are enough to encourage us to continue the journey in search of precious stones for the glorious temple the Holy Spirit wishes to build. Such is the main purpose of this exercise.

B. Going further

As it is written, all the children of Adam are carnal, regardless of where they have lived, unless they have undergone the new birth, which means being born of the Spirit (John 3:6). Otherwise, they will commit errors produced by their feelings and carnal impulses. It was with the object of using the Word of God to make the necessary corrections in the construction of the body of Christ, as an expert architect, that Paul made remarks about the inappropriate behaviors of early Christians. Wherever his counsels apply to the lives of today's Christians, we can apply the writings of Paul to the churches that need them. It should be noted that, in the time of Paul, Greek civilization played a leading role in the world. That is why the Greek language sheds light on certain biblical statements. Carefully scrutinizing these statements, we will have a more accurate perception of certain aspects of the Christian journey. It will give us a close-up image with sharper details. We will feel closer to divine reality.

To begin, let us look together at Ephesians 4:31, which uses three related words: "bitterness," "wrath" (or animosity), and "anger." Paul wrote: "Let all *bitterness*, and *wrath*, and *anger*, and clamour, and evil speaking, be put away from you, with all malice." The Greek for the first word is *pikria*, which means "bitter gall" or "extreme wickedness." The Greek for the other words is *thumos*, which means "anger that boils up and soon subsides," and *orgē*, which means all "anger," the "anger of the natural disposition, temper, character."

I would also like to call your attention to two key terms the apostle used in Romans 1:29, as he admonished believers not to practice, among other things, "unrighteousness," and "maliciousness." In 1 Corinthians 5:8, he warned believers to shun these same two things. These are characteristics that encompass a multitude of undesirable attitudes. They refer to a way of life that comes from the heart. "Unrighteousness" comes from the Greek word *adikia*, meaning "dishonesty" and "that which is contrary to justice or righteousness." Therefore, any unjust action is "unrighteousness." "Maliciousness," or "malice," comes from the Greek word *kakia*, which is derived from *kakos*, the characteristic of a person who seeks to do evil subtly to his neighbor. It is the ability to harm or to do evil in a roundabout way. We are invited to meditate on the obstacles that these behaviors present to the presence of the Holy Spirit in our lives.

Chapter 11

The Christian Soldier

Nearing the end of his life, the apostle Paul likened the Christian journey to the life of a soldier: "Suffer hardship with me, as a good soldier of Christ Jesus. No soldier in active service entangles himself in the affairs of everyday life, so that he may please the one who enlisted him as a soldier. Also if anyone competes as an athlete, he does not win the prize unless he competes according to the rules. The hard-working farmer ought to be the first to receive his share of the crops" (2 Tim. 2:3–6, NASB).

The Soldier's Work

The soldier's job is to wage war and defend the state or kingdom he represents. Paul wrote the Corinthians: "Everyone who enters an athletic contest practices self-control in everything...." (1 Cor. 9:25, ISV). Like the athlete, the soldier must deprive himself of certain moments of leisure and many of the privileges of life that he may devote himself to his military duties. He must train at all times in anticipation of planned and sudden attacks by the enemy army. When you are a soldier, you have become a target. The same is true when you become a Christian. As a soldier, it would be foolish to leave yourself vulnerable to the attacks of the opposing army by removing your soldier's protective clothing, such as a helmet and bulletproof vest. Any stray bullet could take your life. It is best to properly protect and arm yourself with all the soldier's gear. Besides this, you must constantly stay on guard to avoid being surprised. In the Christian life, this means watching and praying with all perseverance. The soldier must train to know his weapons well and to be able to use them in all circumstances.

> *The soldier's job is to wage war and defend the state or kingdom he represents.*

Some people have made the deliberate choice to enter the enemy's camp wearing their uniform without fear of death. In the Epistle to the Hebrews, Paul reminds us that Jesus destroyed Satan's power of death. So those who believe in Him do not have to fear death. "Therefore, since the children have flesh and blood, he himself also shared the same things, so that by his death he might destroy the one who has the power of death (that is, the devil) and might free those who were slaves all their lives because they were terrified by death" (Heb. 2:14, 15, ISV). It is therefore important that every believer be aware that he is enrolled in the army of Jesus Christ and that he or she behave like a soldier under the command of the most powerful commander-in-chief—the LORD of heaven and earth. In the army, rank is given in accordance with a soldier's experience and capacities, taking also into account the competence he has demonstrated in carrying out his duties. In the military, respect for the established hierarchy is essential in maintaining peace and order within the institution. If we transpose this military tradition to the spiritual army that we constitute, it will be a subject of fruitful meditation for us.

Developing Combat Techniques

Soldiers who have acquired greater experience in the art of waging war are more likely to develop effective combat techniques. One can be a devoted soldier with good intentions, yet commit minor errors from a lack of experience. An example of an error of naïveté in spiritual terms is attempting to address Satan directly in a silent prayer, when he cannot hear us.

I have heard the testimony of people who have been attacked by evil angels during a trip or at home. Under such circumstances, prayer, psalms, and songs of praise may be effective. However, we must not forget that

Jesus gives us the power to drive out Satan directly, by commanding him with the authority of Jesus' name. From the enemy's perspective, curses are a prime weapon that he uses against Christians. We vegetate sometimes under the blow of satanic curses, without realizing it, causing us to not be able to keep a job, sustain a marriage, find a partner, go to school, and so on. I heard the story of a taxi driver who drove and drove without any calls for service until someone, who was able to see, told him that no one hailed him for a ride because he always had a person with him in the taxi. In her book *Unbroken Curses*, Rebecca Brown recommends breaking curses in the name of Jesus Christ, whatever their nature. "Christ redeemed us from the curse of the law by becoming a curse for us—for it is written, 'Cursed is everyone who is hanged on a tree'—" (Gal. 3:13, ESV). Not only are we able to break curses in the name of Jesus, but we can also send the evil spirits associated with the curse into the abyss. It is a practical and important subject that concerns us all. It would be profitable to explore it in order to better arm ourselves for spiritual battle.

The Christian's Weapons Are Spiritual

The story is told of a man who was afraid to go to sleep. When it was bedtime, he put a Bible and a sword near his head, reflecting thus: If an assassin comes during the night, I will fight him with my sword. If an evil spirit attacks, I will confront him with my Bible. The humor of his thinking may make some people laugh, but at least he understood that a sword and the strength of his arm would be of no help in fighting an evil spirit. It is the same for all of us who believe in Christ. We need to defend ourselves using all the weapons that God has placed at our disposal. They are known by the names of "truth," "righteousness," "the zeal of the gospel," "the word of God," "salvation," "faith," and "prayer." Later we will talk more about the prayer of faith. Prayer and faith are two powerful weapons that integrate to form an even more formidable multifunctional weapon.

> Finally, be strong in the Lord and in the strength of his might. Put on the whole armor of God, that you may be able to stand against the schemes of the devil. For we do not wrestle against flesh and blood, but against the rulers, against the authorities, against the cosmic powers over this present darkness, against the spiritual forces of evil in the heavenly places. Therefore take up the whole armor of God, that you may be able to withstand in the evil day,

Chapter 11 *The Christian Soldier* 139

and having done all, to stand firm. Stand therefore, having fastened on the belt of truth. (Eph. 6:10–14a, ESV)

Truth is what keeps up all our spiritual defenses. Truth and error are at opposite poles from one another. If everyone holds to his own truth, without concern for the revelation of God's Word (John 8:32; 14:6), then we will miss out on an important offensive and defensive weapon.

… and having put on the breastplate of righteousness, and, as shoes for your feet, having put on the readiness given by the gospel of peace. In all circumstances take up the shield of faith, with which you can extinguish all the flaming darts of the evil one; and take the helmet of salvation, and the sword of the Spirit, which is the word of God, praying at all times in the Spirit, with all prayer and supplication. To that end, keep alert with all perseverance, making supplication for all the saints. (Eph. 6:14b–18, ESV)

Paul's first recommendation is that we fortify ourselves in the Lord, for we will need His strength for difficult times in facing the assaults of the enemy. The enemy has a well-structured organization, of which the apostle speaks in verse 12. Conversely, Colossians 1:16, 17 gives us an idea of the organization of the holy angels of God. "For by him were all things created, that are in heaven, and that are in earth, visible and invisible, whether they be thrones, or dominions, or principalities, or powers: all things were created by him, and for him: And he is before all things, and by him all things consist." According to this text, the organization of the evil angels is modeled after that which is done in heaven. It would be well to review the different weapons mentioned by Paul—truth, justice, the zeal of the gospel, salvation, the word of God, faith, and prayer. These things must not be the work of a moment but the result of a persevering Christian life. The zeal of the gospel calls for our commitment to the work of the Lord. The believer must develop the habit of speaking the truth because the Holy Spirit is the Spirit of truth; He is saddened by lies. The word of God is a mighty weapon. Jesus Christ used it to repel Satan during his temptations. We must also practice rejecting the suggestions of the evil angels by filtering their suggestions through the crucible of the word of God. Faith is required for us to come into possession of the blessings and promises of God. When we ask for something in accordance with the will of God, faith leads us to believe that we have already received what we have asked for. Christians must learn to use this very powerful weapon made available to them. It is both defensive and offensive. It can help us chase the enemy, as it can prevent him from encroaching upon our position as Christians. If this were a book about prayer, we could talk about techniques of prayer based on the word of God. In a fight, experienced soldiers develop techniques to protect and defend themselves and to chase their opponents. The enemy's minions often attack believers on several fronts—visibly and invisibly. Invisible attacks are his usual means of working. Visible attacks are to manipulate the believer in a conflict into creating a breach that will facilitate the success of invisible attacks. For this reason, we must arm ourselves with every spiritual weapon, if we wish to stand firm.

The Power of Our Weapons

"For the weapons of our warfare are not of the flesh, but divinely powerful for the destruction of fortresses. We are destroying speculations and every lofty thing raised up against the knowledge of God, and we are taking every thought captive to the obedience of Christ" (2 Cor. 10:4, 5, NASB). As the weapons we use in this war are not carnal, the carnal man is powerless in this fight. He cannot bring evil thoughts into captivity to the obedience of Christ. We often have the reflex to fight against flesh and blood, that is, against our neighbor. Created good, man was originally incapable of doing harm to his fellowman. Which means that sin is the dominant force that inhabits us and drives us to make bad choices when we have not yet taken possession of all the weapons that God has placed at our disposal. As a result of injustice and misunderstanding, flesh and blood may be wounded, and the weakened warrior may become angry with his fellow man, leaving him vulnerable to manipulation by demonic suggestion to create an antagonist of the one who a minute before was his good friend. After all this, the enemy rejoices in his attack, and the Holy Spirit becomes sad at the failure of love. Paul says that flesh and blood is hostile to God (Rom. 8:7) and that it cannot submit to Him. It is "flesh and blood" that wants to despise, take revenge, and show off. It seeks satisfaction in material things. One Hebrew dictionary connects material things with being "miserable." The reality is that all the needs of our first parents were met when they lived in the presence of God in the Garden of Eden. They lacked nothing. Yet, sin severed this close relationship, and a gaping void was created. We, the children of that first couple, try to fill the void by acquiring things to surround us. Though sin abounds today, we can still take refuge in God through meditation upon His Word, through prayer, consecration, and sanctification, filling our hearts and thoughts with His blessed eternal riches and rekindling communion with Him through the presence of His Spirit.

The state of man's sin has given Satan the right to claim sovereignty over his life. This is why Satan seeks, by all means, to take control of the hearts of human beings, causing them to sink further in sin. Remember Jesus' answer to Satan in his reply to Peter: "Get out of my way, Satan!" (Matt. 16:23, *GOD'S WORD*). We have an obligation to remain in Jesus because Satan constantly patrols the fortress of our hearts to find a breach to enter our lives and to lead us away from our Creator. Satan succeeds when we accept the suggestions he sends us without vetting them by passing them through the crucible of the word of God. In one case, he influences our decisions. In another, he takes total control of a person and even speaks through the one he controls (Matt. 8:29–31). Demons spoke through the demoniacs, asking Jesus to send them into a flock of swine. John wrote: "Whoever makes a practice of sinning is of the devil, for the devil has been sinning from the beginning. The reason the Son of God appeared was to destroy the works of the devil." (1 John 3:8, ESV). The object of sin is to get us to indulge in the practice of sin. The apostle Peter recognized that Christians can still sin because the flesh is still with them, even after the destruction of the "old man" in anticipation of complete redemption. Nonetheless, the blood of Christ is effective in remedying sin. Our heavenly Father wants us to gradually commit fewer and fewer moral offenses as we grow in faith.

Therefore, when we do that which is good, the Holy Spirit is attracted to us; when we do that which is evil, we attract demon spirits into our lives, whose goal is to bog us down in sin. Believers must develop a sharp sense of discernment in their choice of clothes, music, friends, profession, partner, TV shows, websites, films, reading books, decorative paintings for the house, etc. The vast majority of things and activities in the world are made to subtly displace the Creator from our lives and lead us into evil. It is a crucial fact that we obtain spiritual discernment through the working of the Holy Spirit as we are committed to seeking God through engaging in prayer and reading God's Word.

Exploring the Faith

It is the brevity of human life that gives meaning to the passing of time, otherwise one could vaguely observe the alternation of days and nights without worry. As our body wears down with the weight of years, our days are counted and our actions are evaluated in relation to the time that goes away never to return. That is why it is important that we use our time wisely. Every day we see our children growing up before our very eyes while we are preparing to precede them in transitory sleep to await the great resurrection that will coincide with the return of Jesus Christ. Just as love needs time to do its work in the hearts of two lovers to enable the divine equation, $1 + 1 = 1$, to be realized in them, so do we need to spend time with Jesus in a dynamic and loving relation to develop a life of communion with Him. "So faith comes from hearing, and hearing through the word of Christ" (Rom. 10:17, ESV). To understand the true meaning of faith, we must understand our human behavior intellectually, if possible. In addition to the moving of the Holy Spirit in each person's own experiences, God's actions recorded in Scripture must also serve as a catalyst to move us ever forward. In difficulties, we tend to trust the friends with whom we have had positive experiences. It is the same with God. Believers must make themselves available to the service of their God in a spirit of unparalleled commitment and obedience. This is how their faith develops as they walk with their Lord. They will learn to know and trust Him, thanks to the impact of a relationship enriched by revelation.

Our Father in heaven gives every believer the opportunity to experience faith. Yet, faith may seem abstract and volatile so long as it does not produce concrete results. Faith is essential in the life of the Christian, for, without faith, it is impossible to be pleasing to God (Heb. 11:6a), for "a man is not justified by the works of the law but through faith in Jesus Christ" (Gal. 2:16, ASV). It is also by faith that we receive the Holy Spirit (Gal. 3:14). Jesus had described His disciples as people of little faith, asking them, "Why are you so afraid?" (Matt. 8:26, NIV). This He said when He and His disciples were crossing the Sea of Galilee by boat and a sudden storm threw the disciples into a panic while He had been sleeping. Jesus spoke about our worries and anxieties (Matt. 6:25–34). If God has taken care to create us in His image, out of love for us, how will He give more importance to the grass of the fields, which is destined to be dried and burned? "But if God so clothes the grass of the field, which today is alive and tomorrow is thrown into the oven, will he not much more clothe you, O you of little faith?" (Matt. 6:30, ESV). To have faith is to recognize the immensity of something while believing that God in His sovereignty can accomplish a miracle for whom He wills at the moment that He so chooses. Yet, it is undeniably true that faith is also the catalyst for God's miraculous interventions. Because of its importance, it would be beneficial to try to get a handle on this concept.

The experiences of other brothers and sisters can serve to strengthen our faith. In the 1980s, I was visiting a church on a Sabbath morning when the head elder told in a sermon the reasons for his conversion. There had been a boat named Saint-Sauveur [Holy Savior]. It was the connection between the capital and several coastal cities. One day, the ship caught fire off the coast of the town of Dame-Marie [Lady Mary]. The elder heard a brother who did not know how to swim, recount how he survived the episode. Though the boat was destroyed by fire, the brother ended up floating on a board from the debris. As the brother floated, an angel, in the form of a woman, appeared before him on the sea. She engaged him in conversation, asking, "How are you? Have you not seen me when you go to church every Sabbath?"

The brother replied no.

The angel responded: "I see you every Sabbath. I always stand in front of the church door." Then she disappeared.

The brother lay on the board, paddling with his hands to try to reach the shore, which he could see on the horizon. At one point, the board slipped out from underneath him, and he was about to submerge into the deep waters. Yet, he described having the feeling that someone had put him back on the board. He continued to paddle until he reached the shore. The angel reappeared, this time to ask if everything was all right. Then she disappeared once again.

The elder explained that it was after hearing this experience, which touched him deeply, that he made his decision to follow Jesus. This tragedy had struck the whole community. It went beyond the borders of the city. We can imagine the great impact of this experience on the people in the man's neighborhood.

The Significance of Faith

Faith is a firm conviction that relies on God and upon Jesus Christ, on things invisible and spiritual. It is the inner energy of the believer that feeds itself through the word of God and the direction of the Holy Spirit. We may often feel that, at one time or another, faith has remained elusive when we needed it most.

"Now faith is the assurance that what we hope for will come about and the certainty that what we cannot see exists" (Heb. 11:1, ISV). To Hebrews' testimony we can add that of Jesus: "Therefore I tell you, whatever you ask in prayer, believe that you have received it, and it will be yours" (Mark 11:24, ESV). It is necessary to make a mental representation of a desired situation or thing to be able to bring it into existence. For example, if we want Jesus' promises to become a reality in our lives, we must look upon ourselves as children of God and integrate all the virtues that characterize the children of God. Each time we must take action and look at ourselves, saying: We are children of God. Then, we must verify that our actions match up with who we claim to be, to ensure that we are acting appropriately. By faith, the Holy Spirit will help us to embody the characteristics of real Christians. To act in this way is to make a demonstration of the things one hopes for.

> *By faith, the Holy Spirit will help us to embody the characteristics of real Christians.*

Jesus said that He is the vine and that we are the branches. This means that we form the same plant with Him to produce fruits coming from Him. If we integrate this notion into our subconscious and look at ourselves as actually being the branches, the Holy Spirit will produce the transformation in us. Proof of our faith comes when we can pray, when we are aware of God's presence, and when we create within us the actual thing we want to see realized.

Faith can be illustrated by the story of a Christian woman who went to a prayer meeting that was called so they could bring rain. She was the only church member to have the forethought to bring an umbrella. She demonstrated by this act that she believed that the rain would fall at the request of the two or three praying in agreement.

Following our wedding, serious difficulties began to befall my wife and me. A co-worker confessed to me, "The Lord has saved me several times with a strong hand." And now I was going to lose my first child. The difficulty of having another child added to the difficulties that already existed in our lives. To cope with this storm, my wife and I chose to seek divine help through prayer and fasting. One day, a friend who supported us in prayer went to pray on the mountain. There he had a vision: an angel appeared to him with a baby in his arms and asked him this question: "Is it not you who ask a child for John and Mary?"

He answered: "Yes." And, in the vision, the angel tossed him the baby wrapped in a towel, specifying that the baby was a girl. Shortly thereafter, my wife became pregnant with our daughter.

During the pregnancy, my wife had serious concerns about the fetus she was carrying. One night, in a memorable revelation, an angel who looked like a doctor came to consult with her, bringing several pieces of medical equipment connected to a large computer. The angel doctor had a full consult with her, and then he told her that all the results were correct. He gave her a card with his phone number on it, saying, "You can call me at any time with whatever problem you may have." Then the angel doctor was gone.

It often happens in moments of difficulty like this that our heavenly Father seeks to develop a better relationship with us. If we place our trust in Him, by laying all our burdens at His feet, He will bring forth His glory in our lives and will bring astonishing solutions to our anguished hearts when solutions seem impossible. As our experiences with the Lord multiply, our relationship of trust will also increase until nothing can separate us from His love.

Pitfalls to Faith

Doubt is incompatible with prayer. James wrote: "the one who doubts is like a wave of the sea that is driven and tossed by the wind" (James 1:6, ESV). Doubt is a formidable obstacle in the path of believers, preventing them from fully enjoying the spiritual and material blessings of God. Doubt has various sources. It can come from a lack of self-confidence or a past failure. It can be the result of unresolved sin that disturbs our state of consciousness. It may rise from a sin for which we have asked forgiveness yet which we have not been convinced is truly forgiven. Paul invites us to remain firm in the faith, relying on the work of Jesus Christ for us in the heavenly sanctuary. "For we have not a High Priest who is unable to feel for us in our weaknesses, but one who was tempted in every respect just as we are tempted, and yet did not sin. Therefore let us come boldly to the throne of grace, that we may receive mercy and find grace to help us in our times of need" (Heb. 4:15, 16, Weymouth). It is crucial that we do our mental housework to overcome doubt. We must also understand that evil angels are also skilled at the art of making suggestions to bring us failure. In this case, we can refer to the word of God to banish negative ideas in favor of God's promises that can build positive thoughts.

The word of God gives us the assurance that, if we ask forgiveness for a sin for which we have experienced remorse, God will forgive that sin when we forsake it. "If God is for us, who can be against us? Who shall bring any charge against God's elect? It is God who justifies" (Rom. 8:31b, 33, ESV). "And Jesus answered and said to them, 'Truly I say to you, if you have faith and do not doubt, you will not only do what was done to the fig tree, but even if you say to this mountain, 'Be taken up and cast into the sea,' it will happen. 'And all things you ask in prayer, believing, you will receive'" (Matt. 21:21, 22, NASB). Paul wrote: "holding faith and a good conscience. By rejecting this, some have made shipwreck of their faith" (1 Tim. 1:19, ESV). The word "shipwreck" used by Paul brings to mind the catastrophic damaging of a ship that allows water to penetrate it, or, in the case of human beings, that allows a breach into a person's consciousness. It is better to solve problems that could disturb our consciousness and avoid negating the conviction of being pleasing to God. We should not forget that faith is the real demonstration in our mind of the thing we want to possess or the situation we want to see. We must struggle to have peace of mind. Our hearts must be emptied of all sin—including rancor, animosity, falsehood, wickedness, disdain, and vengeance. It is the Holy Spirit who testifies to our spirit concerning the state of our heart.

Our heavenly Father is ready to give us whatever we ask of Him, though we must be aware that He takes His will into account in the process. Believers must verify, through the discernment given by the Holy Spirit in the exercise of their Christian life, whether our request is in accordance with the will of God. It is appropriate to ask for material things in connection with our abilities, yet we understand that money can taint us and prosperity can demonstrate unsuspected qualities. If we allow ourselves to be directed by the Spirit, however, we will be a model of generosity and humility.

The Bible gives examples of some of the servants of the Lord to whom God entrusted great riches without it's preventing them from living in the humility and fear of their Creator. These include Abraham, Isaac, Jacob, Barzillai the Gileadite, Job, and Joseph of Arimathaea.

The Prayer of Faith, a Formidable Weapon

Prayer is a spiritual activity. It is the means that our Creator has placed at our disposal to commune with Him. It would be beneficial, as far as it is possible, to spend a moment singing inspiring songs before praying. By this I mean a song that raises our souls to God. Each one has a few songs that put our mind in touch with the Holy Spirit. The new birth, which is the rebirth of the spirit of man, also has the role of allowing us to enter into communion with our Lord through spiritual prayers. If we pray without being conscious of the real presence of God, to whom we address ourselves, we pray in vain.

Prayer is like a tunnel that we dig to open up a channel to the power of God available on the other side of the hill. This power is unlimited, but the size of our tunnel will determine the amount, or intensity, of the power that will reach us. Jesus told the two blind men who asked Him to have mercy on them: "According to your faith be it done to you" (Matt. 9:29). This means that the quality of our faith determines the extent of the results of our prayers. Prayer is an activity that requires us to invest a great deal of time. Jesus Christ, in whom there has never been a trace of sin, spent considerable time in prayer. What about those of us who are the product of a transplant and not having a pure spiritual nature like Jesus Christ? Time in the western world is a rare commodity. People often try to lengthen their day by appending to the day a part of the night. Yet, the problem is not solved. When time is scarce, despite its constant presence, spiritual activities suffer. It would be more profitable for our mind and body to better plan our time. Jesus taught us about the importance of constancy in spiritual activities such as fasting, praying, and preaching the gospel. It will take time to arrive at our proper destination (see Luke 11:5–13; 18:1–8). We could compare faith to the railway that carries the train of God's power. The condition of the rail is a deciding factor in the train's speed, course, and destination. To Martha, Lazarus' sister, Jesus asked, "Did I not say to you that if you believe, you will see the glory of God?" (John 11:40, NASB). We exercise faith when our mind adheres intensely to the subject of our prayer. This fixation of mind will invite our hearts to join with our minds so that certainty seizes our being.

Back in the 1980s, I had a friend and brother in Christ with whom I sold Christian books during the summer vacation from school. He had become ill and his body was swollen everywhere. He went to the hospital, and a doctor who had studied in Spain diagnosed him with cirrhosis of the liver. He was referred to palliative care. Yet, the brother was not discouraged. He began to pray, saying that he was not going to die because he had not yet finished his work of preaching the gospel. Nonetheless, after several months, the brother went back to the hospital. A doctor had the notion to lance him to remove the water in his body. This simple action led to Brother Paguy's healing. His healing shows, as an example, how the power of God is at work when prayer and faith intermingle effectively.

"The words that I have spoken to you are spirit and life" (John 6:63b, ESV). Jesus' statement means that the word of God can intervene in all facets of our lives. It can cure us of our psychological and physical illnesses. It can save us from danger. It can contribute to success in all our endeavors. It is up to us to believe in the power that resides in God's word.

When negative thoughts bother us, we can get rid of them by reading texts expressing comforting promises, such as—

> Therefore I tell you, whatever you ask in prayer, believe that you have received it, and it will be yours. (Mark 11:24, ESV)

> If God is for us, who can be against us? (Rom. 8:31, ESV)

> I can do all things through him that strengtheneth me. (Phil. 4:13)

> If you had faith even as small as a mustard seed, you could say to this mulberry tree, "May you be uprooted and thrown into the sea," and it would obey you! (Luke 17:6, NLT)

The question resounds in my head: What is faith? According to Mark 11:24 and Hebrews 11:1, faith is a real mental demonstration of the thing hoped for or of the situation that one wants to see take place. There is no doubt that God loves us and that He wants that which is for our good if we have faith. What can prevent our success? If we make use of all the weapons that God has placed at our disposal, who can bar our way? "Verily, verily, I say unto you, He that believeth on me, the works that I do shall he do also; and greater works than these shall he do; because I go unto my Father. And whatsoever ye shall ask in my name, that will I do, that the Father may be glorified in the Son. If ye shall ask any thing in my name, I will do it" (John 14:12–14). I feel that the word "faith" has not given up all its mysteries. I am aware that there are many miracles happening around the world, but we should have done more, according to Jesus' promise.

Chapter 12
An Extravagant Destination

The destination that will be our permanent residence is not comparable to any place already seen or visited on planet Earth. We cannot imagine it or describe it. The benefits of a sincere and devoted friendship is genuine love. Jesus calls His disciples "brothers" and "friends." When true love develops between the Redeemer and the believer, so as to cement their relationship, the believer will feel compelled to pursue the presence of God until this object is achieved. The sensation of alternating closeness and distance, brought about from the earthy and the heavenly, between the flesh and the spirit, drives the believer to seek constantly the perfect balance to maintain God's presence. This incessant quest will keep the believer's love alive as long as he or she lives. This "gearing" of love unfolds at the station where the train that travels towards eternity passes.

The Glorious Return of Christ

Since the establishment of the Christian church, the kingdom of God, in its spiritual and preparatory phase, has coexisted on earth with the system of the world, which has evolved in the opposite direction. The physical establishment of this kingdom on earth has required a long period of transition. This includes not only the passage from a state of sin to a state of holiness on a restored earth but also the gradual transformation of the spiritual man who lives after the divine revelation reached its zenith. As God has unfolded the plan of salvation further, the spiritual darkness of humankind has become brighter, and humans must adjust their spiritual life according to the light received. This individual, contextual change results in the spiritual progress and transformation of the believer in anticipation of the return of Christ. Our spiritual journey is part of a process of gradual transformation that culminates in the completion of the new creation the apostle Paul described in Romans 8:22: "For we know that the whole creation groaneth and travaileth in pain together until now." And we are judged according to the light we have received.

> In the balances of the sanctuary the Seventh-day Adventist church is to be weighed. She will be judged by the privileges and advantages that she has had. If her spiritual experience does not correspond to the advantages that Christ, at infinite cost, has bestowed on her, if the blessings conferred have not qualified her to do the work entrusted to her, on her will be pronounced the sentence: "Found wanting." By the light bestowed, the opportunities given, will she be judged. (Ellen G. White, Ms. 32, 1903, in *Last Day Events*, pp. 59, 60)

A. Prophetic announcements regarding Christ's return

Before His death, Jesus Himself promised that He would return to earth (Matt. 24:30, 31; John 14:1–3). Then, after His resurrection, He reiterated the same promise (John 21:22), and two angels confirmed that promise at His ascension (Acts 1:10, 11).

B. Reasons for Christ's return

Jesus Christ will soon return, according as it is written in His prophetic word, to deliver the kingdom to His Father (1 Cor. 15:24); to reign over the world (Rev. 11:15); to bring to light all that was hidden (1 Cor. 4:5); to judge the living and the dead (Matt. 25:31–46); and to take the elect with Him (John 14:3).

C. Characteristics of Christ's return

The time of this return is unpredictable (Matt. 24:27; Mark 13:35–37). Christ's arrival will be unexpected (Luke 12:40 and 2 Peter 3:10). He will come in the clouds with power (Matt. 24:30; Mark 14:62). His arrival will be visible (Rev. 1:7). It will be accompanied by a great noise (1 Cor. 15:51–55).

D. Promises for the saved

The work of Christ will be fulfilled in the total transformation of the lives of believers (Phil. 1:6; Jude 24). They will be holy and irreproachable (1 Cor. 1:8; 1 Thess. 3:13). They will receive an incorruptible body (1 Cor. 15:42–53). They will bear the image of Christ (Phil. 3:20, 21; 1 John 3:2). They will receive a crown (1 Cor. 9:25; 2 Tim. 4:8; James 1:12). They will reign with Christ (2 Tim. 2:12; Rev. 22:5).

You will notice that I have not drawn up an exhaustive list of the warning signs for Jesus' return but have rather focused on sharing with you the necessary spiritual qualities required by our status as Christians and disciples. It is true that many innocuous events tell us that the return of Christ is near. However, our greater concern should be the state of our spiritual preparation. That has been the purpose of this book: to help readers prepare for Jesus' glorious return.

The True Home of the Believer: The Father's House

The real abode of the human family is their Father's house. Only in the house of the Father can we regain our well-being. The parable of the prodigal son (Luke 15) is an expression of God's love and mercy—in spite of the son's decision to leave his father's home and waste his inheritance. This parable depicts the decline of humanity in its deterioration in quality of life and moral, financial and social standing, once we abandoned our father's house. It is only the presence of God that can direct man towards good. Satan was, in heaven, an angel of light in God's presence. The word of God and our Christian experience show us that, once the human pair was driven from the presence of God after they sinned, the one who had been an angel of light confirmed his status as Satan and has sought to gain control of all humankind. His angelic supporters have been transformed into demons. Deprived of the divine presence, humans have become carnal (Gen. 6:3). Only the presence of God can fulfill all the needs of the human heart. In the Garden of Eden, Adam and Eve lacked nothing. Yet, God's absence in the life of human beings has created a lack manifested by multiple needs. When God is absent, our carnal impulses push us to covetousness.

The void that is created in each person's life is proportional to the distance that separates him or her from the presence of God. Thus, the degree of the void varies from one person to the next, depending on whether that person is approaching or moving away from the divine presence. The Hebrew language, recognized as the language of divine expression, is instructive. The Hebrew word *Abah*, meaning "to be willing," "to consent" is the root for the Hebrew word *Ebyown*, or *Ebion* (translated "poor" in Ps. 132:15), which means "miserable," "needy," or "poor"—marking the lack of all things necessary for life. Some argue that the *Ebionites* were so classified because of their "poverty of intelligence." It can also mean a person who continually desires the things necessary for life. Thus, fallen human beings have become miserable and needy, for they need the vain and futile things under the sun to satisfy the clamor of their heart.

> *The void that is created in each person's life is proportional to the distance that separates him or her from the presence of God.*

Another Hebrew word worth exploring is *hebel*, which means "vanity." In Jeremiah 2:5, the Lord asked His people why they have abandoned Him to follow after vanity, or "futile things" (*hebel*)? The word *hebel* also means "steam, breath, futility, nothingness." As Ecclesiastes opens, Solomon pronounces the book's refrain: "Vanity of vanities… all is vanity" (Eccles. 1:2, 14; see also Eccles. 2:17; 3:19; 12:8). In chapter 2, he added: "the work that is wrought under the sun is grievous unto me: for all is vanity and vexation of spirit [chasing the wind, NIV]" (Eccles. 2:17). Solomon was a king without peer; he knew glory; he had great wealth. However, his wisdom enabled him, in the final analysis, to compare all that he had to the greatest of vanities. At the time that King Solomon lived and reigned, his fame as the wisest man extended beyond the borders of his country. Dignitaries from across the globe came to meet him to see for themselves what they had been told. To better understand the king's sentiment, it is important to ask: What is true wisdom? What is its source?

The record of Scripture includes the story of a man who is a myth for some and reality for others. That man lived around the second century BC, and answered to the name of "Job." This man, who lived in this remote period of the history of this world, was wise enough to ponder the origins of wisdom. Without wisdom itself, it would not have been possible for him to have observed that, unlike many other things in life that have

Chapter 12 *An Extravagant Destination*   153

great material values, the source of wisdom is hidden in God and must be approached spiritually. Wisdom preceded man; at no time was it lacking. In a monologue that ends in an appeal, Job points the way to acquire this exceptional virtue.

> "People know where to mine silver and how to refine gold. They know where to dig iron from the earth and how to smelt copper from rock. ... They sink a mine shaft into the earth far from where anyone lives. They descend on ropes, swinging back and forth. Food is grown on the earth above, but down below, the earth is melted as by fire. Here the rocks contain precious lapis lazuli, and the dust contains gold. ... People know how to tear apart flinty rocks and overturn the roots of mountains. They cut tunnels in the rocks and uncover precious stones. They dam up the trickling streams and bring to light the hidden treasures.
>
> "But do people know where to find wisdom? Where can they find understanding? No one knows where to find it, for it is not found among the living. 'It is not here,' says the ocean. 'Nor is it here,' says the sea. It cannot be bought with gold. It cannot be purchased with silver. It's worth more than all the gold of Ophir, greater than precious onyx or lapis lazuli. Wisdom is more valuable than gold and crystal. It cannot be purchased with jewels mounted in fine gold. Coral and jasper are worthless in trying to get it. The price of wisdom is far above rubies. Precious peridot from Ethiopia cannot be exchanged for it. It's worth more than the purest gold.
>
> "But do people know where to find wisdom? Where can they find understanding? ...
>
> "God alone understands the way to wisdom; he knows where it can be found, ... And this is what he says to all humanity: 'The fear of the Lord is true wisdom; to forsake evil is real understanding.'" (Job 28:1, 2, 4–6, 9–20, 23, 28, NLT)

If everything on earth is nothing but vanity, then human beings, in order to find happiness, must take refuge in the presence of God. The readiness to make wise decisions is found nowhere but in the fear of the Lord. Such fear will lead us to the Father's home. This is what He offers us through the unfolding of the plan of salvation. Chapter 21 of Revelation allows us to gain a glimpse of the preparations being made for the new abode of God with His children. Let us pray and work to hasten the moment when the New Jerusalem descends from heaven to re-establish the atmosphere of Eden between God and humankind.

> *Chapter 21 of Revelation allows us to gain a glimpse of the preparations being made for the new abode of God with His children.*

The New Jerusalem

Then I saw a new heaven and a new earth, for the first heaven and the first earth had passed away, and the sea was no more. And I saw the holy city, new Jerusalem, coming down out of heaven from God, prepared as a bride adorned for her husband. And I heard a loud voice from the throne saying, "Behold, the dwelling place of God is with man. He will dwell with them, and they will be his people, and God himself will be with them as their God. He will wipe away every tear from their eyes, and death shall be no more, neither shall there be mourning, nor crying, nor pain anymore, for the former things have passed away."

And he who was seated on the throne said, "Behold, I am making all things new." Also he said, "Write this down, for these words are trustworthy and true." And he said to me, "It is done! I am the Alpha and the Omega, the beginning and the end. To the thirsty I will give from the spring of the water of life without payment. The one who conquers will have this heritage, and I will be his God and he will be my son. But as for the cowardly, the faithless, the detestable, as for murderers, the sexually immoral, sorcerers, idolaters, and all liars, their portion will be in the lake that burns with fire and sulfur, which is the second death."

Then came one of the seven angels who had the seven bowls full of the seven last plagues and spoke to me, saying, "Come, I will show you the Bride, the wife of the Lamb." And he carried me away in the Spirit to a great, high mountain, and showed me the holy city Jerusalem coming down out of heaven from God, having the glory of God, its radiance like a most rare jewel, like a jasper, clear as crystal. It had a great, high wall, with twelve gates, and at the gates twelve angels, and on the gates the names of the twelve tribes of the sons of Israel were inscribed—on the east three gates, on the north three gates, on the south three gates, and on the west three gates. And the wall of the city had twelve foundations, and on them were the twelve names of the twelve apostles of the Lamb.

And the one who spoke with me had a measuring rod of gold to measure the city and its gates and walls. The city lies foursquare, its length the same as its width. And he measured the city with his rod, 12,000 stadia. Its length and width and height are equal. He also measured its wall, 144 cubits by human measurement, which is also an angel's measurement. The wall was built of jasper, while the city was pure gold, like clear glass. The foundations of the wall of the city were adorned with every kind of jewel. The first was jasper, the second sapphire, the third agate, the fourth emerald, the fifth onyx, the sixth carnelian, the seventh chrysolite, the eighth beryl, the ninth topaz, the tenth chrysoprase, the eleventh jacinth, the twelfth amethyst. And the twelve gates were twelve pearls, each of the gates made of a single pearl ... (Rev. 21:1–21a, ESV)

This chapter allows us a glimpse of the indescribable place that the saved will live. All this is a foretaste of eternal paradise, a glimpse of the wonderful things God has prepared for His elect.

> ... and the street of the city was pure gold, like transparent glass. And I saw no temple in the city, for its temple is the Lord God the Almighty and the Lamb. (Rev. 21:21b–22, ESV)

The twenty-first chapter of Revelation opens a window on the reality of what will come after the return of Jesus Christ. It is a glimpse of what the eye has not seen and the ears have not heard. The new Jerusalem will descend from heaven, a splendid city dressed as a bride ready for her wedding. We will no longer suffer the silence of God, since He will share His tabernacle with us. This is a passage to read as we make our pilgrimage on the earth, for it speaks of expectancy, hope, renewal, joy, peace, and love. From the day of our birth, we live side by side with despair, disappointment, conflict, suffering, sickness, war, pain, death, and mourning. This next-to-last chapter of sacred Scripture projects us into a new perspective. He reassures us that all these things and their bad memories will disappear forever. I try to imagine this glorious day. We shall be seized with a childish joy, unbridled and real. In verse 5, Jesus Christ took care to emphasize that these revelations are "trustworthy and true."

Exploring the New Jerusalem

The angel accompanied by the apostle John continues the exploration of the city. The city, with its magnificent splendor, reflects the glory of God. The number twelve, which has long integrated our Christian reality—between the twelve tribes and the twelve apostles—is the basis for all the dimensions of the eternal city. The names of the twelve disciples will be engraved for eternity in the most prestigious gallery of art in the universe, erected under the sign of the number twelve. All of those whose sacrifices will be rewarded in this way will have their names engraved eternally in the eternal sanctuary of God and man. Certainly Paul's name is inscribed there, like the name of the disgraced woman who anointed Jesus' feet with her expensive perfume in the house of Simon. The criteria for receiving divine honor and glory are not social, economic, or intellectual. They are on a wholly different basis than the world of our senses in which we now live. Divine honor and glory rely on a spiritual assessment of each person, according to divine criteria focused on *agapē* love, humility, service, and obedience. "For God does not show favoritism" (Rom. 2:11, NLT).

Surpassing the red carpet rolled out to receive human dignitaries and celebrities, Jesus has laid out a golden street for us, and He will give us a warm embrace, whispering in our ears words of commendation for glorifying His name under difficult circumstances. There will be plenty to enjoy besides living an idyllic life in an environment of perfect happiness. The angel continues the description of the heavenly city with its cubic dimensions.

> And the city has no need of sun or moon to shine on it, for the glory of God gives it light, and its lamp is the Lamb. By its light will the nations walk, and the kings of the earth will bring their glory into it, and its gates will never be shut by day—and there will be no night there. They will bring into it the glory and the honor of the nations. But nothing unclean will ever enter it, nor anyone who does what is detestable or false, but only those who are written in the Lamb's book of life. (Rev. 21:23–27, ESV)

Let us notice certain important characteristics of the city: There will be no night; the glory of God will be its light; the Lamb will be its lamp; the doors of the city will always remain open; the Lord God is His Temple; the city has twelve gates of pearls; and the main street of the city is pure gold that looks like crystal. The twelve foundations of the wall are constructed using twelve different precious stones. The number twelve and some of its multiples represent certain measures in the main dimensions of the city and its essential elements.

The beginning of the last chapter of Revelation speaks of a crystal-clear river that supplies the city with water. In the middle of the city, on both sides of the river, rises the tree bearing fruit twelve times a year, the leaves of which serve for the healing of the nations. Finally, the throne of God and the Lamb will be in the city, and His servants will see Him face to face. The angel does not forget to reaffirm in verse 6 that these words are certain and true, and the Lord, the God of the spirits of the prophets, sent His angel to show His servants the things that are soon to happen. The question we have to ask ourselves is: If there were now a city like this on earth, or in some other place accessible to humankind, who could remain there or even go there for a visit or for a vacation? With it being on this planet it will be possible to go there and stay forever—without paying a cent—for all the expenses are already paid by Jesus Christ!

BIBLIOGRAPHY

Bible d'étude Semeur

Bivin, David and Roy Blizzard, Jr. *Understanding the Difficult Words of Jesus.*

Brown, Rebecca. *Unbroken Curses.*

Canfield, Jack, Mark Victor Hansen, Marci Shimoff, and Carol Kline. *Chicken Soup for the Mother's Soul II.*

Chaij, Fernando. *Preparation for the Final Crisis.*

Frendelvel, José. *L'or des Étoiles: Nouveau regard sur le système solaire* [The Gold of Stars: A New Look at the Solar System], 2005.

Kreeft, Peter. *The God Who Loves You.*

Kuen, Alfred. *Les lettres de Paul: introduction au Nouveau Testament* [The Letters of Paul: Introduction to the New Testament].

Leigh, Le Chevalier and Louis de Wolzogue. *Dictionnaire de la langue sainte* [Dictionary of the Holy Language].

Nouveau Testament interlinéaire grec-français [The Interlinear Greek-French New Testament].

Pache, René. *The Inspiration and Authority of the Bible.*

--------. *The Person and the Work of the Holy Spirit.*

Pasquier, Thierry. *Le Guerrier Intérieur* [The Inner Warrior], pocket edition.

Peale, Norman Vincent. *The Power of Positive Thinking.*

Pigeon, Eugene Richard. *Dictionnaire du Nouveau Testament* [New Testament Dictionary].

Thompson's Study Bible.

Trench, Richard C. *Synonyms of the New Testament.*

Vigouroux, Fulcran. *Dictionnaire de la Bible* [Bible Dictionary], vol. 5.

White, E. G. *The Desire of Ages.*

--------. *Last Day Events.*

--------. *Steps to Christ.*

TEACH Services, Inc.
P U B L I S H I N G

We invite you to view the complete
selection of titles we publish at:
www.TEACHServices.com

We encourage you to write us
with your thoughts about this,
or any other book we publish at:
info@TEACHServices.com

TEACH Services' titles may be purchased in
bulk quantities for educational, fund-raising,
business, or promotional use.
bulksales@TEACHServices.com

Finally, if you are interested in seeing
your own book in print, please contact us at:
publishing@TEACHServices.com
We are happy to review your manuscript at no charge.

www.ingramcontent.com/pod-product-compliance
Lightning Source LLC
Chambersburg PA
CBHW070554160426
43199CB00014B/2501